JAMES G. MARCH
AND THIERRY WEIL

ON
LEADERSHIP

Blackwell
Publishing

French edition © 2003 by École des mines de Paris, Paris
English edition © 2005 by James G. March and Thierry Weil
Translation copyright © 2005 First Edition Translations Ltd

BLACKWELL PUBLISHING
350 Main Street, Malden, MA 02148-5020, USA
9600 Garsington Road, Oxford OX4 2DQ, UK
550 Swanston Street, Carlton, Victoria 3053, Australia

The right of James G. March and Thierry Weil to be identified as the Authors
of this Work has been asserted in accordance with the UK Copyright,
Designs, and Patents Act 1988.

Originally published in 2003 by École des Mines de Paris as
Le leadership dans les organisations
English edition published 2005 by Blackwell Publishing
Translation by Matthew Clarke for First Edition, Cambridge, England

1   2005

Library of Congress Cataloging-in-Publication Data

March, James G.
On leadership / James G. March and Thierry Weil.
p. cm.
Translated from French (originally a set of unpublished lecture notes in
English by James March, interpreted in French by Thierry Weil)
Includes bibliographical references and index.
ISBN-13: 978-1-4051-3246-6 (hard cover : alk. paper)
ISBN-10: 1-4051-3246-9 (hard cover : alk. paper)
ISBN-13: 978-1-4051-3247-3 (pbk. : alk. paper)
ISBN-10: 1-4051-3247-7 (pbk. : alk. paper)
1. Leadership—Study and teaching.   2. Leadership in literature.
I. Weil, Thierry.   II. Title.

HD57.7.M3919 2005
303.3′4—dc22
2005004896

A catalogue record for this title is available from the British Library.

Set in 10/12.5pt Adobe Garamond
by Graphicraft Limited, Hong Kong
Printed and bound in the United Kingdom
by TJ International Ltd, Padstow, Cornwall

For further information on
Blackwell Publishing, visit our website:
www.blackwellpublishing.com

CONTENTS

FOREWORD:
THE GENIUS OF MARCH

The thinking of March is disconcerting.

James March enjoys a reputation as an immense source of wisdom with respect to the social sciences and, as a result, writers in this field routinely pepper their work with quotations from his œuvre. How, though, should his work be classified? In terms of disciplines, his subject matter and contributions range from the sociology of organizations to political science, from management to economics. Furthermore, in a world that relishes its division into schools or paradigms, March cannot be pinned down, but he nevertheless provides inspiration to all and sundry: some of his colleagues, although not short of their own ideas, turn to his work to boost their own creativity. His drive for knowledge can be dizzying, but he instils skepticism in upholders of so-called normal science as his contributions defy any attempts to pigeonhole them. As for many publishing houses, although the name of James March is an emblem of prestige, the contents of his books present as extremely heterodox and the financial risk is considered too great for an author that does not fit the template of a best seller.

Is March's thinking really grounded in a scientifically watertight approach? One can be forgiven for doubting this at times. This book by James March and Thierry Weil discusses art. March has also dared to publish books of poetry, which are marked by their sensitivity and depth. This leads us to conclude that he is, above all, an impenitent aesthete and sophisticated hedonist, for whom social science is not the be-all and end-all of life. March's scientific activities – writing articles and conducting rigorous analysis – are not restricted to his professional sphere; likewise, his love for music and literature extends beyond his personal life and leisure time. For March, science and art are in a constant, mutually enriching relationship.

March's thinking is normally associated with terms that are now common currency in social science: neo-institutionalism, the garbage-can model, attention focus, organized anarchy, etc. If these expressions are examined more closely, it becomes apparent that they are closer to metaphor than solid concepts, and the exploitation of metaphor is typical of poetry. Although it serves an important function, metaphor is underused in scientific work; it can be justified, however, by its capacity to question the validity of received ideas, render postulates explicit, and criticize the theoretical models lurking behind them. Art enables scholars to bring their intuition into play, thereby giving rise to new interpretative and conceptual schemes. Poetry, literature, and music act as stimuli for grasping and analyzing facts. A metaphor, therefore, is intrinsically neither true nor false – its value is judged in the light of its ability to further knowledge.

On Leadership calls on suitable metaphors to understand the workings of human enterprises. It offers a stunning demonstration of stubborn nonconformity, filtered through the rereading of great works of literature. It shows March in action, as a discoverer constructing more effective interpretative systems in a world otherwise distinguished by provisional truths and evasive clichés. This book by March and Weil is therefore required reading for anybody whose profession involves the diffusion of knowledge, while also reflecting the rebellious spirit that informs and shapes March's work.

March's course challenges the assumptions that dominate today's institutions – those of the MBA. It offers a scientific and intellectual approach to teaching large bodies of students in establishments as standardized as business schools and, in particular, it reinforces its case with classical plays and novels. Imagination and nerve are required to bring off this feat successfully.

I have repeatedly found that company bosses cultivate a secret garden: the study of famous works and classical authors focusing on the art of warfare and leadership in battles. Clausewitz, Sun Tse, Epaminondas, and Napoleon get them thinking, spurring them on to confront competitors, dream up strategies, formulate tactics, and rally their troops on the battlefield. The ideas propounded by management studies strike them as extremely simplistic by comparison, as well as being remote from the realities of the business world.

March and Weil's book draws on works that are less militaristic in tone but nevertheless forged in passion and fury. By asking his students to read Cervantes, Shakespeare, and Tolstoy, March introduces a note of provocation and stages an act of rebellion.

James March is not partial to making critical denunciations in a public arena. If a situation appears scientifically unsound, or if an idea strikes him as morally untenable, he prefers to keep his own counsel at first, but sooner or later he will reply, basing his arguments on his work in social science. This is why his rare ripostes, although polished and measured, strike with so much force.

In one sense, *On Leadership* is a means through which March and Weil respond to their intellectual and institutional concerns. The course that sowed the seeds for this book is a teacher's solution to a problem of scholarship. The methods that currently predominate in business schools are both faced with, and victims of, a dangerous contradiction.

These schools promise professional courses that educate future business people by means of scientific knowledge, particularly that related to social science. More recently, however, this knowledge has been imparted less and less, especially in the past 20 years. Training via research has been replaced by training via cramming. In class, future MBA graduates receive little more than instruction, which is dispensed by "trainers" and solely geared to "training." Science and the logic of research have deserted – or been banished from – the classroom. The school is reduced to operating as the instrument of the labor market. It has become the seminary of the business community: it selects and certifies graduates, propagating and legitimizing the values and norms endorsed by the business world.

This trend is fomented in a number of ways. Students are force-fed formalized models, strong indicators, and procedural tools. They are imbued with an image of the world and action that encourages certainty, prescriptive measures, and the predominance of the manager-designer. Excellence is reduced to the formulation of solutions. Students are taught to act through conditioned reflexes; learning how to think becomes secondary. Knowledge – dealing as it does with an uncertain world, weak indicators, incremental action, heterogeneous rationality, variable and specific contexts, and responsible appropriation of the consequences of actions – struggles to survive in these training factories. Free and creative thinking barely gets a look in; students assimilate ready-made thinking and actions.

It is not the least of the merits of March and Weil's book that it reminds managers of some profound truths, including the fact that leadership has no unanimously accepted wellspring.

If we are to believe current thinking, the issue of leadership has been resolved. The best of all worlds comes into view when, and only when, a leader-boss guides and supervises a group to which he or she has supplied a vision or destiny, and to which he or she serves as the common denominator or emotional and regulatory point of reference. In politics, business, and private life, a distinctive factor makes all the difference: the leader is ultimately a phenomenon associated with outstanding personal qualities rather than circumstances, contexts, or organization. The consultants and business trainers have not mistaken their market. They rush to offer products with titles that explicitly refer to leadership. There is a plethora of ads touting creative or dynamic leadership.

What a turnaround! The period from the 1960s through the 1980s was marked by the triumph of the organization, the quest for scientific rationality, and the belief in procedures and techniques. Today, excellence is expected from the actions of exceptional individuals and seen in virtues such as charisma and intuition.

It is easy to stress the extent to which such a viewpoint is debatable and vulnerable to attack. Leadership remains a hazy subject when seen from the perspective of social science. What is to blame for this – the incompetence of researchers, or the fact that the word attempts to designate an essentially intangible phenomenon? What is certain is that the training industry recycles, sometimes with blatant opportunism, materials and techniques whose link to leadership is not readily apparent: 360 degrees, group dynamics, etc.

This book by James March and Thierry Weil broadens our understanding of this topic in a masterly fashion. It refocuses the spotlight on moral dilemmas and private life; it discusses power and enthusiasm; it suggests that, in order to pinpoint the essence of leadership, we must go beyond the narrow definitions of social science. Although the authors take many liberties, they do so in a responsible manner – they are neither *provocateurs* nor essayists, but educators guided by research.

Jean-Claude Thoenig
INSEAD
DRM, University of Paris Dauphine

PREFACE

This book is about leadership. The topic is a contemporary publishing cliché. It is hard to imagine anything except the conceits of the authors and the overconfidence of the publishers that would generate another book on leadership. Without denying either the conceits or the overconfidence, I hope that this little volume might be justified both by its modest size and by its relatively unusual genesis and character.

The book is based on lectures given and queries posed in a course I taught at Stanford University from 1980 to 1994. The course was based on three primary convictions. The first was that the major issues of leadership were indistinguishable from issues of life. A proper discussion involved reflecting on grand dilemmas of human existence as they presented themselves in a leadership context. The second conviction was that great literature was a primordial source of learning about such issues for educated people. An inquiring, skeptical, and tolerant gaze was cast on leadership, primarily through a lens provided by four great works of literature – *Othello* by William Shakespeare, *Saint Joan* by George Bernard Shaw, *War and Peace* by Leo Tolstoy, and *Don Quixote* by Miguel Cervantes. The third conviction was that education, including education in business schools, should not attempt to furnish students with recipes or prescriptions for success. Education was seen in a more classical spirit, as helping humans to consider ways to understand the essential dilemmas of human existence and the essential nature of the human spirit. These heroic aspirations were, of course, never fully achieved in the course; but their pursuit provided a certain protection from the grim pursuit of immediate relevance that sometimes plagues business education.

The book is also unusual in the manner of its authorship. The text is an English translation, by Matthew Clarke, of a French interpretation, by Thierry Weil,[1] of a set of my English-language lecture notes. The original lecture notes were truly notes, not finished essays, thus they required the fine French hand, not to mention audacity, of Thierry Weil (a French physicist, student of organizations, and former advisor to the French Premier). As he observed in his introduction to the French interpretation of the lecture notes, recreating lectures you did not yourself attend on the basis of a professor's elliptical notes, is a tricky affair. He described the effort as "motivated by the desire to preserve a trace, albeit a very blurred one, of a work that was original in both its substance and its teaching methods." I do not know whether the desire should be commended, but I am grateful for its pursuit.

The job was formidable. The lecture notes covered twenty, 75-minute lectures and were 450 pages in length. Although the notes were voluminous, they were incomplete and underdeveloped, and the lectures they engendered varied from time to time. Translating them into a manageable book involved simultaneously reducing them greatly and elaborating them selectively. Thierry Weil, who had previously written a book on my contribution to the study of organizations,[2] took on the task – without, I assume, realizing at the start what might be involved. With only a few minor exceptions, the words in the book are his (as translated from the French by Matthew Clarke).

The book does not always respect the detail and sequencing of the sections of either the course or the lecture notes, nor does it give attention to each theme proportional to that displayed by the notes or the course. The chapters in the book move rapidly over topics that have been extensively explored elsewhere in my published work in order to deal more fully with the unpublished ideas. For example, the discussions of decision making, learning, and risk taking in organizations comprise a smaller proportion in the book than in the notes, and the discussions of gender and sex a larger proportion.

In order to keep the book a decent size, Weil also eliminated a number of extended discussions found in the lecture notes that dealt with things

[1]   J. G. March and T. Weil, *Le leadership dans les organisations*, © École des mines de Paris, Paris, 2003, ISBN 2-911762-50-9. Dépôt légal: décembre 2003 Ecole des mines de Paris, 60, Boulevard Saint Michel, 75272 Paris Cedex 06, France.
[2]   Thierry Weil, *Invitation à la lecture de James March*. Paris: Les Presses de l'École des Mines de Paris, 2000.

that would have required extensive explanation. For example, the lecture notes (but not the book) include a long discussion of romance novels in the context of talking about gender and power. They contain discussions of W. B. Yeat's poem, *Easter 1916* in the context of talking about Irish revolutionaries and arbitrary commitments. They contain extended treatments of T. S. Eliot's poem, *The Love Song of J. Alfred Prufrock*, and of *The Saga of Olav Trygvasson*. At the same time, Weil also includes several topics that were not featured in the lecture notes, but which seemed to him to be particularly relevant, in order to illustrate, for example, my ideas about the selection and reputation of leaders, or the way to run efficient organizations.[3]

In a general way, the book describes leadership as less heroic and less significant to history than is common in books on leadership. It explores some ways in which a fuller understanding of the relationships between individual well-being and the status and behavior of leaders will help the latter to come to terms with their ambitions, their obligations, and their frustrations; help others to appreciate, support, and resist leadership; and help a society to define roles for leaders that are both socially useful and personally gratifying.

The interpretations developed by Thierry Weil are faithful to the spirit of the lecture notes, but they neither provide complete explication nor reproduce the lectures exhaustively or precisely. The text is often elliptical, with arguments more suggested than developed and with connections often left to the imagination. As a result, the chapters in the book should be read more as prose poems than as normal essays.

The lack of any serious protest to or revision of the French text on my part speaks to Weil's success in combating the risks of false interpretation. A similar thing can be said about this English translation. I have added a few words sometimes organized into a few sentences, but basically the voice remains Weil's. For me, the movement of ideas from English to French and back to English is not only thoroughly charming but constructive and possibly even creative. As Weil pointed out in the French version of the

---

[3] James C. March and James G. March, "Performance sampling in social matches," *Administrative Science Quarterly*, 23 (1978) 434–53; J. Richard Harrison and James G. March, "Decision making and post-decision surprises," *Administrative Science Quarterly*, 29 (1984) 26–42; "Mundane organizations and heroic leaders," lecture by James March in Mexico in 1988, printed here as Appendix 2 and published in a French translation in *Gérer et Comprendre*, June 2000; "Les mythes du management", lecture by James March to the École de Paris du management, June 1998, *Gérer et comprendre*, September 1999.

book, this relaxed acquiescence on my part is not entirely devoid of ambiguity. I believe that a written piece belongs as much to its readers as to its author, and that the meanings readers discover in a text are likely to be at least as interesting as those in the author's mind. In this case at least, there is more evocation than corruption in the production of an English translation of a French interpretation of some English lecture notes, and I am grateful to Thierry Weil for his creativity, to Sally Heavens and Matthew Clarke for the translation, and to Blackwell editor Rosemary Nixon for her tolerance.

James G. March
Stanford University

As recalled by James March, this book is an attempt to preserve a trace, even a very blurred one, of a course that has deeply impressed many classes of Stanford students and scholars, and was original in both its substance and its teaching methods, but had never been put in a published form. It was meant to share with others part of the enjoyment I had in discovering the abundant multifaceted work of Jim March, mainly through his writing, and in too rare occasions through attending some of his seminars, talks, and open discussions. I was openly hoping that Jim would be so exasperated by my oversimplistic report on his work that he would feel compelled to restore the truth and eventually write a book on leadership, despite his resistance to reducing a colorful and buoyant performance into a flat linear text. It would not have been without glorious precedent: even Cervantes was driven to write the second volume of *Don Quixote* after the publication of an apocryphal, mediocre sequel. I did not succeed in this gross manipulation. To my consolation, however, Jim wrote a short paper (extensively quoted in chapter 1) on "Literature and leadership." Much more significantly, while this book was on its way, he wrote the script and narrated a film, *Passion and Discipline* about the lessons of Quixote (and I hope that he and Steve Schecter, the film producer, will succeed in getting another one made about *War and Peace*).

Because of its topic, this book is not only a tribute to James March, but also to my father, who was my first example of a leader and who worked and endured without profit to himself to provide me with the psychological, intellectual, and material opportunity of not having to follow, regardless of the cost, a traditional career. It is also a tribute to some managers that I had the chance to meet in many different settings, as well as to all those who contribute in very obscure but essential roles to the effective functioning of organizations. It is finally, by its very topic, a tribute to the poets, inventors, dreamers, and friends, who by their works, their deeds, and the humanity of their existence, enrich and embellish our lives.

Thierry Weil
École des Mines de Paris

CHAPTER 1

INTRODUCTION

Issues of Leadership

The fundamental issues of leadership – the complications involved in becoming, being, confronting, and evaluating leaders – are not unique to leadership. They are echoes of critical issues of life more generally. As a result, they are characteristically illuminated more by great literature than by modern essays or research on leadership. Consider, for example, the following small handful of central issues:

Private lives and public duties:[1] Leaders have private lives from which they draw emotional balance and human sustenance, though they often find their official lives systematically more rewarding. Leadership can destroy both the privacy and the quality of personal life. The importance of position undermines authenticity in personal relations. Self becomes inseparable from standing, thereby making love and hate equally suspect. Leadership also attracts curiosity and gossip, compromising privacy. Followers claim a right to knowledge about a leader's personal life on the grounds of its relevance to assessing character and establishing rapport. Finally, private lives complicate the responsibilities of leadership. Personal motives and relations affect the actions of leaders. Personal jealousies and loyalties bend a leader's judgment. Interpersonal trust contributes to, yet corrupts, organizational actions. What are the possibilities for combining a rich personal life with

---

[1] This theme is explored, for example, in Shakespeare's *Othello*, as we shall see in the next chapter, and, in French literature, in *Bérénice* by Racine and *Horace* and *Le Cid* by Corneille.

life as an organizational leader? How are personal feelings to be reconciled with organizational responsibilities?

Cleverness, innocence, and virtue:[2] Commentators on leadership are ambivalent about sophistication and cleverness. On the one hand, leaders are often portrayed as astute manipulators of resources and people, praised for their use of superior knowledge and adroitness. They are frequently described as intelligently devious and secretive, as wily experts in maneuver and misdirection. We honor their superior abilities to outsmart others. On the other hand, leaders are often pictured not as sophisticated in the usual sense, but as possessing an elemental innocence that overcomes the fatuous convolutions of clever people and goes instinctively to the essentials. This capability for simplification is associated not with education, intelligence, and propriety but with an ability to connect, in some uncomplicated way, to the fundamentals of life. In this spirit, leaders are often praised for their naïveté and openness, and for their ability to use honesty as a basis for inspiring and extending trust. What is the place of cleverness and innocence, intelligence and ignorance in descriptions of, or prescriptions for, leadership?

Genius, heresy, and madness:[3] Great leaders are often portrayed as geniuses. They are said to see further and more accurately than others. Because of this visionary capability, they dare to take risks that others dare not. They transform organizations through their imagination, creativity, insight, and will. These descriptions of great leaders seem, however, to portray greatness as being associated with heresy, thus to be at variance with the needs of organizations for safer, more reliable behavior. The needs are not perverse. Though heresy sometimes proves, retrospectively, to be the basis for desirable change, most bold new ideas are foolish and properly ignored. They are more likely to destroy an organization than to lead it to new heights of achievement. Thus, great leaders are characteristically heretics who are associated with a transformation of orthodoxy, but most heretics would be disasters as leaders. What are the relations among genius, madness, and leadership? How do we recognize great leaders among the crazies? How do we nurture genius if we cannot recognize it before history does?

---

[2] This theme is explored, for example, in Shakespeare's *Othello* and *King Lear*, Machiavelli's *The Prince*, *Dirty Hands* by Sartre, and *The Just Assasins* by Camus.

[3] *Saint Joan* by George Bernard Shaw, *Mithridate* by Racine, *Doctor Faustus* by Thomas Mann.

Diversity and unity:[4] In everything from problem solving to personnel policies to ideologies, leaders make trade-offs between diversity and unity, between variety and integration, between convergence and divergence. Organizations are collections of individuals and groups often having quite diverse attitudes, backgrounds, religions, aspirations, training, identities, ethnicities, experiences, social ties, and styles. Leadership frequently involves finding ways to minimize the problems of diversity through recruitment from a common background, experience, or education, or through the use of persuasion, bargaining, incentives, socialization, and inspiration to mold multiple talents and backgrounds into a common culture. Such a vision of leadership as forging a unity of harmonious purpose and commitment clashes, however, with an alternative vision of leadership as stimulating and nurturing diversity as a source of organizational innovation and social strength. How do leaders choose between building unity and building diversity? Can they have both? To what extent is unity at one level in an organization a necessary precondition for diversity at another?

Ambiguity and coherence:[5] Leadership is generally seen as a force for coherence, as contributing to effective organizational action by eliminating contradictions and preventing confusions. Future leaders are taught to remove inconsistencies, ambiguities, and complexities through precise objectives and well-conceived plans. The modern prototype in a business firm is the idea of business strategy and the development of a "business plan." However, inconsistency and ambiguity have a role in change and adaptation, and the compulsion toward coherence could be an incomplete basis for understanding or improving leadership and life. In general, effective leadership implies an ability to live in two worlds: the incoherent world of imagination, fantasy, and dreams and the orderly world of plans, rules, and pragmatic action. How do we sustain both ambiguity and coherence? Both foolishness and reason? Both contradiction and resolution? To what extent are talents to do so related to artistic, literary, and poetic imagination?

Power, domination, and subordination:[6] Many modern ideologies treat inequalities in power as illegitimate. Yet, we pursue power and are fascinated by it. We equate personal power with personal self-worth, and powerlessness with loss of esteem and identity. We write history and describe

---

[4] *The Ugly Duckling* by Andersen, *Frederick Prince of Homburg* by Kleist.
[5] *War and Peace* by Tolstoy, *The Charterhouse of Parma* by Stendhal.
[6] *Zero and Infinity* by Koestler, *The Devil and the Good Lord* by Sartre, *The Saga of Olav Trygvason* by Snorre Sturlson, *Dilbert* by Scott Adams.

progress in terms of changing patterns of domination and subordination. As a result, we see power as both central to leadership and a complication for it. We recognize a tension between hierarchy and participation, between power and equality, and between control and autonomy. Power is often said to corrupt the holder of it, to transform normally honorable people into monsters. It is also said to condemn, to undermine the ordinary pleasures of honesty in interpersonal relations. At the same time, power is often described as elusive, more a story-telling myth than a reality. Insofar as leaders have power, how do they use it? What are its limits? What are its costs? How does a person with little power function in a power-based institution? What are the moral dilemmas of power?

Gender and Sexuality:[7] Gender and sexuality are well-recognized factors in modern biology, sociology, and ideology. They affect a wide range of behaviors, and interpretations of behaviors, in organizations. In virtually all societies, leadership is linked to questions of sexual identity and gender equality. Historically, most leaders have been men; and the rhetoric of leadership has been closely related to the rhetoric of manliness. Changes in gender stereotypes with respect to leadership interact with the ways women and men are interpreted to have (or not have) distinctive styles, characters, beliefs, or behaviors, as well as with our understandings of their relations, not only outside hierarchical organizations, but also within them. Moreover, leadership appears to be intertwined with sexuality. Being a leader and being seen as having power are components of sexual appeal and sexual identity. Sexual relations and accusations of sexual misconduct are endemic around leadership. How do the manifest elements of sexuality and gender in leadership affect the ways we understand, become, and act as leaders?

Great actions, great visions, and great expectations[8] The ideology of leadership emphasizes reason more than foolishness, strategy and vision more than serendipity and improvisation, thinking more than imitation. Action is seen as intentional, driven by an evaluation of its expected consequences. Costs are paid because benefits are anticipated. Within such an ideology, leaders need to have expectations of great consequences to justify the great commitments demanded of them. They need to believe they can make a difference. We ask whether this is an adequate description of leadership behavior or an adequate moral foundation for it. In particular, we examine the implications of justifying great actions by great hopes in a world

---

[7] *Dangerous Liaisons* by Choderlos de Laclos.

[8] Miguel de Cervantes, *Don Quixote*; Fyodor Dostoyevsky, *The Idiot*.

in which causality is obscure and effectiveness problematic. Within an ethic of consequentiality, how do we sustain commitment in the face of adverse or ambiguous outcomes? How do an organization and a society maintain illusions of efficacy among its leaders? What are the consequences? Are there alternatives?

Pleasures of the process:[9] Leadership and leaders are generally justified and understood in instrumental terms. We see leadership as contributing to the ways in which organizations are coordinated and controlled to improve outcomes. Leaders evaluate themselves, are evaluated, and are (to some extent) compensated in terms of their contributions to those outcomes. At the same time, it is frequently noted that there are pleasures associated with the processes of leadership: the glories of position, the joys of commitment, the excitements of influence, the exhilaration of conflict and danger. These pleasures are, to a substantial extent, independent of their outcomes. As a consequence, understanding leadership often involves recognizing the ways in which the pleasures of the process fit into the calculus of leadership and how they ought to do so. What are the major pleasures of being a leader? How do they affect recruitment into leader roles and behavior within them? How do they affect the way we think about leadership?

The proper texts for discussing these fundamental issues of leadership are drawn from Shakespeare, Molière, Ibsen, Tolstoy, Cervantes, Mann, Goethe, Akhmatova, Schiller, Stendhal, Kawabata, Shaw, James, Dostoevsky, Balzac, and others of similar stature. Great literature engages these questions in a deeper and more enduring way than other texts. This greater engagement stems from a more profound realization that the issues are to be seen as intractable dilemmas rather than as problems to be solved. They deal with what the great Danish physicist, Niels Bohr, called "profound truths" – recognizable by the fact that their opposites are also profound truths. Because the struggles with these truths have no resolution, they create enduring inter- and intra-personal conflicts; and understanding them involves experiencing the social, personal, and intellectual pains of those conflicts.

We must be aware, however, that the relevance of great literature to the understanding of the problems linked with leadership must not be seen as its primary justification. Reading great books is an end and a pleasure in itself. Rereading them in a particular light makes it possible to escape from

[9] Francois Rabelais, *Gargantua and Pantagruel*; Isabel Allende, *Aphrodite: A Memoir of the Senses.*

the tradition of analyses that focus on other aspects of a work, as one of the characteristics of great literature is that it gives rise to a host of interpretations, but can never be reduced just to these.

Michel Zinc, Professor of Medieval Literature at the *College de France*,[10] remarked to an association of students' parents in the summer of 2002:

> leaving aside any ideas about careers, literary culture makes life so agreeable! It enhances our capacity to enjoy it so much! Being capable of reading and finding pleasure in a book, even a slightly difficult one, that resonates with the most serious issues, the ones we think about without being able to find an answer to them, that spin around inside our head continuously; because we cannot progress on our own; and so in the course of a book – a book that generally does not claim in any way to provide a direct answer to these issues, a book that can be a novel or a poem – we say "Good Lord! That's exactly right," and we extend the book with everything that we bring to it and we extend ourselves with everything that the book brings to us.

Appreciation of Leadership

The objective is to appreciate leadership, not in the sense of glorifying it but in the sense of being fully aware of it on the basis of sensitivity and understanding. The appreciation of leadership, like the appreciation of music, art, or literature, is constructed on a foundation of knowledge and girded by a point of view. It is a way of engaging experience, a way of creating, elaborating, and embracing an aesthetic of experience. It draws from the same human instincts and capabilities as the understandings of science, or the insights of poetry, or the truths of art and music, or the elaborations of expertise of any kind.

Appreciation involves the creative tensions of comprehension, tensions between the observations of life and the metaphors of life. In science, those tensions are between observations and theories. In art, the tensions are between representation and interpretation. In self-discovery, the tensions are between experience and consciousness. The great geniuses of those tensions include philosophers such as Kierkegaard and Unamuno, poets such as Wordsworth and Goethe, writers such as Doestoevsky and Ibsen, and social scientists such as Darwin, Marx, and Freud. It is an ancient

[10]   The College de France, founded in 1530 by King Frances I, is a place where the only duty of appointed scholars is to teach at least one fully original public course every year.

tradition and, as such, contains considerable potential both for pretentiousness and for inanity.

The focus is on the appreciation of leadership. It is a familiar focus. Much of our conversation about leadership is evaluative. We evaluate individual leaders, assessing their reputations for having done well or having done good. Reputations are typically not self-evident. There is often ambiguity about outcomes and their attractiveness. There is ambiguity about who is responsible for the outcomes. As a result, reputations are social constructs negotiated among observers, accountants, journalists, academics, leaders, competitors, friends, and enemies. Reputations diffuse through a population of observers and often change over time.

We also evaluate leadership as an idea and a reality. Just as Bertrand Russell said "It is not appreciation of the artist that is necessary so much as appreciation of the art," we might say that it is leadership that is to be appreciated, not the individual leader. What beauty and ugliness can we discover in the existence, practice, and consequences of leadership? We interpret the place of leadership in life. That interpretation often distinguishes two important kinds of features of leadership. On the one hand, leadership has an instrumental role. It is implicit in the most common technology of organizing – the hierarchy. At the same time, leadership has a symbolic role. It is an important element in our interpretations of history and experience. It is tied to ancient mythic stories that frame modern understandings.

The results of such a focus fill modern media. History is pictured as being the result of intentions and actions of leaders. Biographies of leaders are a steady element of lists of best selling books. These writings develop notions of the role of leaders in society, on the attributes of leaders, and on the relation between being a leader and being a proper person. They create a language of leadership, a language filled with ideas of vision, power, and virtue.

Leadership appreciation, like music or art appreciation, involves combining a distinct perspective with ordinary knowledge to produce greater insight. It involves an awareness of paradox, the recognition of simultaneous (and not necessarily consistent) feelings and analyses, and a commitment to intellectual playfulness. But most of all, it involves an acceptance of leadership and leaders. This does not mean a commitment to approval, but it does mean a fundamentally positive, unalienated perspective. Just as great pieces of art criticism involve seeing things of value in art different from what others may see, leadership appreciation involves seeking an interpretation of leadership that ennobles, rather than demeans, its subject. It is an ambition far too grand, but it is nonetheless the ambition.

An appreciation of leadership depends, first of all, on *a view of the human estate – a conception of the role of individual human beings in the nature of things.* Leadership is implicated in human ambitions for control over their histories, and any interpretation of leadership proceeds from basic ideas about the centrality, or lack of it, of human beings in the order of things. It also proceeds from some conception of the dependence of a good life on personal success. How important is success relative to the autonomous dignity of the self? To what extent are good and evil knowable? What is the significance of the inevitability of short tenure and death? And it proceeds from an attitude about innocence. To what extent is human victory possible? What are human capabilities for knowing virtue? What is the likelihood of virtue being rewarded in a terrestrial life? To direct a discussion of leadership into concern for such issues is to embed it hopelessly in extraordinarily difficult questions, and yet they cannot be ignored.

Second, an appreciation of leadership depends on *a view of social organization – a conception of the bases for justifying governance and differentiation.* It evokes echoes of Plato, Aristotle, Aquinas, Rousseau, Locke, and Madison. It depends on ideas of justice and representation. For many, the justification of any particular social organization depends on three quite different questions.

The first is the *technical* question: Does the system discover and implement mutually attractive exchanges of resources? Is it efficient? The great claim of market-like systems is the claim (more powerfully demonstrated in theorems than in observations but to some extent in the latter) that it locates Pareto-preferred distributions of resources.

The second question is the *political* question: Are power and resources distributed justly? The classic justifications for inequality in the distribution of power and resources lie in differences among individuals in the impact of governance on them and in their contributions to social well-being. The more one is affected and the more one contributes, the greater the legitimacy of the possession of power and resources. Even where such justifications are accepted, organized systems have persistent difficulties stemming from disparities between the boundaries of the systems (in space and time) and the distribution of their effects.

And the third question is the *moral* question: What contribution does the system of governance and differentiation in power and resources make to virtue and the good life? To what extent do they create or sustain attractive human beings or an attractive human existence?

Is the proper basis for organization ideas of bilateral exchange in which individuals are imagined to be blessed with preexistent preferences and exogenously determined resources and imagined to make mutually satisfactory exchanges through deals, trades, and markets? Or is the proper basis for organization a structure of rules and institutions with their preexistent conceptions of the obligations of personal and social identities? Or is the proper basis for organization a conception of community dominated by a search for a shared destiny and institutions for shaping preferences, feelings, and senses of wisdom? Different conceptions lead to different metaphors of leadership – military metaphors, market (broker) metaphors, administrative metaphors, political metaphors, consensual metaphors, parental or educational metaphors, and trustee metaphors.

Third, an appreciation of leadership depends on *a view of social action – a conception of the bases for action in life, particularly in organizations.* To an overwhelming extent, contemporary ideologies of action within theories of choice see action as instrumental, coherent, and justified subjectively. Action is instrumental in the sense that it is taken intentionally and is based on expectations of future consequences for the objectives of the actor. Actors are intendedly rational. Action is coherent in the sense that goals and alternatives are well-defined and the decision rule is clear. Actors choose from among alternatives by calculating and comparing their expected returns. And the justification for action is subjective. It is assumed that the value an individual associates with a particular outcome cannot be compared meaningfully with the value another individual associates with a particular outcome. There is no interpersonal comparison of utilities. Values, thus, are assumed to be irrefutable.

Many of the central themes in discussions of leadership echo these conceptions. Leadership is pictured as demanding great action, thus as requiring great expectations. Leaders are praised for making intelligent instrumental choices, criticized for failing to do so. At the same time, however, such a conception of action has been subject to criticism. Students of organizational behavior observe that organizational goals are often ambiguous, inconsistent, and changing. The experiences of history are hard to interpret and often misleading or unclear. The power of a leader is ambiguous, as are success and failure. Students of action observe that calculated, instrumental rationality is not the only basis for human action. Human behavior has often been described as stemming less from calculations of consequences than from the fulfillment of an identity, a logic of appropriateness rather than a logic of consequences. Moreover, such a basis for action has been praised as resulting in more deeply human, even more effective, actions.

Finally, an appreciation of leadership depends on *a view of self – a conception of oneself, of a proper individual's response to the nature of things.* How do we think of ourselves? Are we self-interested optimizers? Are we identities seeking opportunities to fulfill the expectations of our roles? Are we citizens seeking community? How do we react to the fundamental features of an ordinary life? How do we react to the asymmetries of life, to variations in success, rewards, and power? How do we react to the ambiguities of life, to lack of clarity about the world, history, and desires? How do we react to contradictions and dilemmas? How do we deal with the absurdities of life, with the reality of mortality and the impermanence of the species? How do we balance a personal life with the demands of our surroundings?

Such issues evoke the great conflicts of life: A predilection toward equality and modesty versus an urge to power and self-assertion. A commitment to rationality, instrumentality, and the pursuit of self-interest versus a conception of duties, obligations, and the pursuit of justice. A desire for clarity, integration, coherence, and unity versus a propensity to ambiguity, inconsistency, and conflict. A claim of human significance versus an awareness of human absurdity and mortality.

The present notes are in the tradition of the human struggle to confront such issues. It is an honorable tradition, but one that should be followed only with trepidation. Any discussion of the issues is inevitably incomplete. They are the things of which life is made and experienced and cannot be comprehended or solved. Since the earliest attempts to create a human canon, they have been food for the ruminations of philosophers, novelists, biographers, and poets – all unavoidably aware of their meager capabilities relative to the task.

Queries

The "queries" presented at the end of each chapter are a sample of those used in the course at Stanford. They were used to provoke thinking and discussion and to provide bases for short written essays. They were not guaranteed to reflect the attitudes or beliefs of the instructor.

1.1

Contemporary enthusiasms for university courses and curricula in leadership, for executive development seminars on leadership, and for books about leaders are a continuation of a long-term fascination with leaders and leadership that infects historians, journalists, novelists, biographers, and story tellers of all sorts. There are two basic theories of why the fascination endures:

1. Leaders and leadership are, in fact, important; history is shaped by the actions of individual leaders. According to this theory, we believe leaders are important because they are.
2. Although leaders are, in fact, unimportant, social conventions dictate that stories of history be organized around the actions of leaders. According to this theory, we believe leaders are important because that is the way history is told, and history is told that way because we expect and want it to be.

Both theories are plausible, but it is not easy to choose between them on the basis of empirical observations. Most of the evidence adduced to support the first theory can also be used to support the second, and vice versa. Nevertheless, each has enthusiastic and persuasive supporters.

Why do the theories gather support? Who would be more likely to be enthusiastic about the first theory? Who would be more likely to be enthusiastic about the second? What are the implications for leadership?

1.2

The fundamental difficulty with discussions of leadership is that they accept a false premise. The false premise is that leadership is something positive to put on a personal résumé. In fact, leadership is something of which one should be rather more ashamed than proud. Most disasters in organized life can be attributed to leaders, and being a leader has corrupted more people into leading unattractive lives and becoming unattractive selves than it has ennobled.

The problem doesn't lie with the people who have become leaders. They are not really different from others. The problem is with the concept of leadership. It is based on a premise of the nobility of command that has repeatedly been proven to be false. The giving and taking of commands may on rare occasions be justifiable – just as taking a life may be – but it is always destructive of the human spirit.

Comment.

1.3

Nothing significant about leadership is likely to be said by people who have been leaders. People who have been leaders are no more capable of an intelligent appreciation of leadership than Americans are of appreciating the American experience, men are of appreciating masculinity, artists are of appreciating art, or the elderly are of appreciating old age. Comprehension requires the passivity of indifference. Interpretation requires the perspective of distance.

Comment.

1.4

Modern leadership is preeminently organizational leadership and requires talents quite different from those of mythic heroes. The kinds of postures and dramatics that typify classical heroes might solicit a kind of nostalgic enthusiasm if found in a minor player, but they would produce laughter or revulsion rather than allegiance if exhibited by a significant leader in the current day.

Moreover, the major crises of modern life are not organized around the classical issues of heroic mythology. Instead, they are crises of self. Modern heroes are not warriors who overcome external threats but individuals who overcome personal battles with drugs, alcohol, and degradation. As a result, the traditional association of leadership and heroics has become largely irrelevant to understanding contemporary heroes and contemporary leaders.

Comment.

CHAPTER 2

DUTY, REVENGE, AND INNOCENCE: *OTHELLO*

Private Life and Public Duties

From the earliest division of work to Weberian bureaucracy, our society has progressively dissociated the public role and the private sphere. We can see this either as the alienation of individuals, who are only partially fulfilled in either of their roles, or, on the contrary, as their liberation, leading them to exist independently of their function in the group and transcend it. Individuals are not limited to what they must "render unto Caesar" or alienated by the logic of capitalist production.[1] They are accountable for their actions in the public sphere and free to indulge their tastes in the private one. They will be judged on the basis of equitable and objective criteria in a meritocratic society rather than on the basis of status at birth or contacts.

Work does in fact often represent a major part of our social identity.[2] In the contemporary western world relationships based on contracts (economic relations) have increased in importance relative to relationships based on senses of belonging (family, group, nation). "The market" has invaded the private sphere: our preferences are manipulated by advertising and the benefits of political institutions and agencies are seen as consumption goods

---

[1] Professor Claude Riveline points out that, in the Egyptian bas reliefs, the figures are all represented in exactly the same way and are only distinguished by the attributes of their function. Rendering unto Caesar the things that belong to Caesar would, therefore, be a way of appropriating all the rest and confirming the preponderance of the individual over the role.
[2] This is illustrated, conversely, by the loss of self-esteem and confidence experienced by the unemployed and by some retired people, even in the absence of financial difficulties.

rather than aspects of citizenship. Some tasks that were once the respons-ibility of parents are now easier to delegate or farm out. The Weberian separation of the public and private spheres, invented in a male profes-sional world, is called into question by the increasing influence of women more reluctant (or less able) to leave their family responsibilities at home.

There are other interactions between the private sphere and public life. Private life is a vital source of personal enrichment and regeneration for the practice of a public role. It can also contribute to a reputation, or con-stitute a source of corruption, when friendships or membership of a com-munity impinge on professional decision-making.[3] Reciprocally, public life affects private life: a status-enhancing public role is a source of material well-being, prestige, and self-confidence, yet is also a threat to private life and the authenticity of human relationships.

Moreover, public life involves emotional engagement. The professional sphere is a source of accomplishment, of psychological gratification, of demands (duties connected to function, moral obligations to clients or their representatives), of intimacy (in comparison to an intrusive family life), and of rich and affectionate human relationships.

Finally, in both the private and public spheres, the roles are multiple, complex, and composite. The individual can be torn between different, poten-tially conflicting identities (public and private ones, particularly those connected to family, ethnic group, religion, and community).

Leaders allocate their time according to the demands imposed by their objectives, the expectations of the people with whom they come into con-tact (linked to habits and affinities), what they have learned from experience, and sometimes even rational assessments. All these reasons drive them to work hard, especially if they take the challenges of their position seriously. As a result, their private lives are likely to be entwined with their public lives, making their senses of themselves often dependent on their public per-formances and fates.

---

[3] It should be noted that what may appear as a corruption of a rational order based solely on merit can constitute a factor of efficiency in fields where trust is a fundamental element in the running of a business. Membership in a community increases the cost of opportunistic behavior and the guarantee derived from the importance of keeping up a good reputation. It therefore represents a rational element, albeit an inequitable one, that should be taken into account in selection. The public role can therefore be facilitated by certain private alle-giances: so, for example, Henry IV of France pragmatically converted to Catholicism to secure power, reasoning that "Paris is well worth a Mass."

The public demands (particularly in the United States) to know about the private life of leaders to verify whether they have the moral characteristics needed to inspire trust (e.g., Bill Clinton and the Monica Lewinsky affair). Some people delve into a leader's private life in order to establish a better personal relationship with him or her. What salesman does not want to know about the hobbies of his client, and what employee does not gain favor by indulging the tastes and fads of his or her boss? Intimacy only has value, however, if it is confined to a privileged, inner circle. Finally, the social pressure exerted on a leader to expose his or her private life is a mixture of a desire for conformism (constituents want a leader to be predictable and so discard any deviants), a demand that a leader should be an example to others, and the hypocrisy of sinners happy in the knowledge that a leader is no more virtuous than they are.

In the face of these contradictory pressures, we can imagine several systems of equilibrium:

- *The eunuch system*, where the leader gives up the right to a normal private life, as in the case of modern monarchs, trapped by a stifling etiquette, or workaholic bosses who forego all personal pleasure to devote all their energy to business.[4] But are they really "eunuchs" or are they camouflaging hidden, private ambition? Are these the people that we want to see exercising power?
- *Predatory leaders* who aim to satisfy their private ambitions (a careerist driven by the desire to predominate, a Mafia boss). But do they have the requisite support and sense of obligation? Are they good leaders? Is it possible to have confidence in an "invisible hand" to guide and control competition between grasping individuals to a satisfactory social outcome?
- *The Weberian schizophrenia between the public role and private life.* But do they not impact on each other? And do the people who best come to terms with such a dichotomy make the best leaders?

On the whole, Othello fits into the first category, considering that public duty takes precedence over private pleasure and that no friendship could corrupt his conduct as a leader:

---

[4]   So, in the Wagnerian myths, Wotan, Alberich, and Klingsor must give up love in order to reign over the world.

> Cassio, I love thee,
> But never more be an officer of mine, (II, 3)

and:

> [When . . .] That my disports corrupt and taint my business,
> Let housewives make a skillet of my helm,
> And all indign and base adversities
> Make head against my estimation. (I, 3)

Othello accepts that in order for a leader to be worthy of his function, he must have an irreproachable personal reputation. He admits that if he were guilty of having seduced Desdemona wrongfully, as Brabantio accuses him of doing, then he would be unworthy of his leadership position. His obligation of respectability extends to his entourage and a transgression by Desdemona would disqualify him. At the same time, Othello thinks it normal that his public merits should earn him private rewards, such as the right to marry above his status at birth, or outside his racial group.

Revenge and the Social Order?

Othello embodies an aristocratic concept in which the possession of power imposes an obligation to pursue an exemplary private life, but in which public merits justify private gratifications that include ennoblement and higher social status.

This aristocratic conception can be contrasted with a conception of a social order based on the competition of opportunists seeking primarily to satisfy their ambitions and their desires rather than contribute to the common good (predatory leaders rather than eunuchs). In this scheme, the equilibrium of terror based on the threats of retaliation by those who consider themselves unjustly treated establishes a certain degree of equity.

Iago speaks for such a conception. Notwithstanding the murkier aspects of his character, Iago boasts a moral justification. His desire for revenge is initially presented as a need for equity, as Iago suspects that Othello has seduced his wife Emilia:

> For that I suspect the lusty Moor
> Hath leap'd into my seat: the thought whereof

Doth, like a poisonous mineral, gnaw in my inwards;
And nothing can or shall content my soul
Till I am evened with him, wife for wife
Or failing so, yet that I put the Moor
At least into a jealousy so strong
That judgment cannot cure. (II, 1)

In a system guided by such considerations, revenge restores the equilibrium of exchange between individuals, thereby guaranteeing the social order. If a grievance is not redressed (either because the victim and the guilty party cannot agree on a fair compensation, or because the damage cannot be compensated), the victim may claim the right to inflict damage on the guilty party in return. This possibility of revenge, as long as it is credible, discourages affronts and therefore serves the cause of justice. Revenge is a motivation that is all too rarely discussed, but it is essential to an understanding of certain aspects of life within organizations.[5]

Revenge is, however, too unstable a foundation for an enduring order. Individuals have their own subjective appreciations of the value of a good deed or an offense and can therefore have difficulty in reaching agreement about what is fair; in addition, the motivations that come into play may be highly irrational. Ambition is insatiable, so its aspirations alter in line with what has already been obtained; therefore, any "equilibrium" of terror always involves a risk of escalation. In order for the equilibrium to remain stable, there must be a certain tolerance of "slightly" inequitable situations (for example, being ready to invest three-quarters of the capital and only

---

[5] The desire for equity is not rational, to the extent that it can drive people to act against their own interest. This is illustrated by the game "Ultima," involving two players who do not know each other, do not communicate with each other, and will have no subsequent interaction. The first chooses how much he or she will keep out of a sum of 100 dollars, and how much he or she will give to the second player. The latter can choose between accepting the split or withdrawing from the game, in which case neither player will receive any money at all. Game theory predicts that it is in the interest of the first player to propose a share-out that is strongly in his or her favor (for example, leaving the second player only a few dollars and pocketing the rest) as this unbalanced distribution will always be "better than nothing" for the second player and the two players will have no further interaction. Most second players, however, turn down share-outs that are too inequitable (depriving themselves of profit in order to punish the first player, whom they do not even know and in whose education they have no interest at all), and most first players anticipate this behavior by proposing reasonably well-balanced share-outs.

reap a quarter of the profits) and no individual should overestimate the threat represented by others in the organization.

Confronted with an ambiguous reality, the economics of revenge rest on a choice between two risks of error: that of believing a guilty person to be innocent (false negative) or of believing an innocent person to be guilty (false positive). In this spirit, Othello recognizes that it would be only to his advantage to convince himself of Desdemona's innocence, even if she were guilty:

> What sense had I of her stolen hours of lust?
> I saw't not, thought it not, it harmed not me;
> I slept the night well, fed well, was free and merry;
> I found not Cassio's kisses on her lips.
> He that is robbed, not wanting what is stol'n,
> Let him not know't, and he's not robbed at all. (III, 3)

The paranoid (or jealous) individual, however, prefers to punish an innocent party rather than leave the guilty one undisturbed:

> **IAGO**: I know not if't be true
> Yet I, for mere suspicion in that kind,
> Will do as if for surety. (I, 3)

> **DESDEMONA**: I never gave him a cause.

> **EMILIA**: But jealous souls will not be answered so;
> They are not ever jealous for the cause,
> But jealous for the're jealous. It is a monster
> Begot upon itself, born on itself. (III, 4)

Despite the dangers of an outburst, is revenge sometimes a legitimate instrument of regulation in organizations? How would we judge Othello if we knew that Desdemona was guilty of treachery? And are we, the spectators who condemn Othello's foolishness, not frustrated by Iago's impunity?

Whether it is legitimate or not, revenge has an essential place in the life of leaders, as they:

- are exposed to the desire for revenge of those under them;
- are often manipulated to serve as instruments to settle other people's scores;

- can use organizations to carry out their own revenge; and
- also have the function of controlling other people's instincts for revenge.

Cleverness, innocence, and virtue

Theories of action   The example of the desire to avenge a real or imaginary affront shows us the complexity of the motivations for human
actions and their ambiguous impact on both the aims apparently pursued
by an individual and the regulation of organizations. Let us dwell on this
point for a moment before considering another aspect of Shakespeare's play,
the destabilizing of the relationship between the gullible Othello and the
virtuous Desdemona by the ruses of the perfidious Iago.

Our understanding of the actions of individuals or organizations is often
influenced by various myths and interpretations of the world that determine what we think of as true, beautiful, and just. More specifically, the
observation of human actions raises two fundamental questions:

1. *What are the bases and motivations for action?* Why do people do what
    they do and how do they justify it? We can invoke a consequential-
    ist logic (achievement of individual or collective aims), a logic of affinities
    (players act in accordance with their individual identities or construct
    the latter through their actions), or finally a logic of faith and arbitrari-
    ness, which stands apart from the economic viewpoints of the ratio-
    nalists and the socio-psychological ones of the logic of affinities and
    identity: as Kierkegaard wrote, a religion that seeks to justify itself instru-
    mentally is no longer a religion.
2. *What is the fundamental character of the game?* Is it played against an
    exogenous nature? Can we assume that the actor knows and analyzes
    the situation perfectly and that the results of his or her action are pre-
    dictable? Or is it a game against other strategic actors? What are the
    rules about permissible falsifications and violations of agreements?

The answers to these questions lead us to distinguish the four major branches
of action theories (see Table 2.1):

- *Decision theory*: the player is rational and plays against nature (which
  is known, at the very least, in the form of distribution of probabilities);
  the decisions that are taken are put into practice;

Table 2.1 Four major branches of action theories

Basis of the action \ Opponent	Nature	Other players
Rationality	Decision theory	Game theory
Identity (and rules)	Institutional theories	Ecological theories

- *Game theory*: the player is rational and plays against other players, whether rational or otherwise, within a framework of legal or social conventions;
- *"Institutional" theories of action*: the players act against nature in accordance with their identities, following rules fixed in a system of generally accepted norms; and
- *"Ecological" theories of action*: the players act in accordance with their identities and follow certain rules of the game, playing against players who are following the same rules although these can evolve over time (co-evolution of the players and the rules).

In an ecological vision, we can distinguish between two types of players: *clever ones*, who act solely in their own interests – assuming that the other players are doing the same – and are opportunistic, self-confident, and users of complex strategies; and *innocents*, who act in accordance with obligations or affinities (often interiorized as instinctive virtue), trust the people around them, and favor transparent strategies.

The fundamental myth is one of individuals who were initially innocent (Adam and Eve in the Garden of Eden), but have been corrupted by their encounter with clever opportunists (the serpent, a second-hand car salesman, an intellectual, or a professor) who caused them to lose their innocence (teaching them to distinguish Good from Evil, or sending them to a business school to learn how to calculate discounted present values). When history is moral, God intervenes to damn both corruptor and corrupted: the professor is condemned to remain a professor, to read the *Wall Street Journal* and *New York Times* every day, and to make subtle, intellectual constructions that are obscure and far-removed from reality, while the fallen innocent must work and ceaselessly run after possibilities of promotion right until the day that he or she is fired by the organization.

Do we expect a good leader to be clever or innocent? Being clever involves a worldview in which every player pursues individual interest, a virtuous action is one that is effective, and the end justifies the means, with God rewarding the toughest by allowing them to survive – unless He simply bestows the gift of cleverness on those He loves. In this scheme, we admire the wily politician who achieves personal ends at the expense of gullible fools, the crafty negotiator, and manipulator. We would glorify Othello for having used a subtle maneuver to deceive the Turkish fleet about his intentions and the distribution of his ships in order to launch a surprise attack and win victory. A world in which everyone seeks to be clever is not, however, a very attractive prospect: the costs are onerous for the losers and for society as a whole (e.g., defending against opportunism devoid of faith or law and the defiance of other people). In this case, the long term is often sacrificed for the short term, the faraway for the close at hand, as in countries that have an overly "clever" foreign policy or corporations that cheat their partners or clients.

Being innocent involves a worldview in which people are naturally good, virtue is based on a clear knowledge of Good and Evil or, at the very least, on simple actions ("let us cultivate our garden"), God rewards virtue, and history is marked by human progress. Innocence can be a result of naïveté in the face of the vicissitudes of the world or a voluntary decision to promote a better world by ignoring evil and arbitrarily opting for trust and love. So, we admire the "Boy-Scout" leader who gets things done through stated principles and the instinctive wisdom of a man of the people. We only tolerate cleverness when it is crowned with success, while the failure of innocence is attributed to the perversity of the world. Nevertheless, it is not enough merely to demand innocence of a leader. We condemn the military commander whose troops have committed atrocities, because he is morally culpable if he knew about them and unworthy of his command if he did not know (because he should have). The road to Hell is often paved with good intentions and virtuous actions do not always lead to temporal rewards. Don Quixote and the character of Pierre Bezukhov in *War and Peace* are just two examples of this. Furthermore, it is difficult, on an emotional level, to rely on the benevolent judgment of others (or of history) on the basis of premises that one knows to be false and thereby appear naïve to one's inner circle.

What happens in a world populated by a mixture of clever and innocent people? In one standard morality/evolutionary tale, at first, the clever ones dominate and exclude the innocents from all positions of power. The distinctions between the powerful very quickly become tenuous, however, as only the clever have survived and cleverness no longer represents a decisive advantage in a competitive situation. The few deviants who remain worthy of confidence now become rare and much sought-after allies and find themselves associated with victorious coalitions. This does not lead to a stable equilibrium, however, as, when a society of trust is established once again, opportunistic behavior can become worthwhile. Opportunism often brings immediate advantages, in the short term or in the local vicinity, while innocence brings benefit on a long-term basis or to a more widespread community – always providing that the innocents survive for long enough.

Leaders must therefore reconcile innocence and cleverness. The short term leads them to be clever, but it is also in their longer-term interest to construct good reputations by avoiding cleverness. Building a reputation of trustworthiness can be difficult, however, and the fact that behavior is innocent is not always sufficient for it to be credible. Consider Brabantio, to Othello, pointing out his daughter Desdemona:

> Look to her, if thou hast eyes to see;
> She has deceived her father and may thee. (I, 3)

The characters in *Othello*   The interplay between private and public and the tensions between cleverness and innocence are exemplified by the major characters in the play.

Othello – who subordinates his private life to his public duties, and whose public reputation (which depends on his military glory, but also on the behavior of his wife) determines the vision he has of himself – finds himself confronted by the self-interested cleverness of Iago and the generous pragmatism of Emilia, as well as the innocence and unconditional love of Desdemona. In that confrontation, Othello has reasons for being vulnerable to a paranoid jealousy. He has used his prestige to seduce and win the daughter of a senator. Although Venice had sufficient need for his talents as a general to embrace the union, Othello knows that that support goes against the prejudices of the society and is fragile.

Iago, a plebian on the rise, the spirit of the Enlightenment, extols the triumph of the will over the passions: "Our bodies [feelings] are our gardens, to which the wills are gardeners . . . but we have reason to cool our raging motions, our carnal stings, our unbitted lusts; whereof I take this that you call love to be a sect or scion" (I, 3).

His ambition is to climb the social ladder, if necessary by pushing other people down it – a zero-sum situation in which one person's gain is necessarily someone else loss. He is affronted by Othello's choice of Cassio as his lieutenant. He dreads appearing a dupe or cuckold (but that is also the lot of Othello, Roderigo, Brabantio, and Emilia). The fact that Iago is him-self pathologically jealous (he suspects Othello, but also Cassio) fuels his desire for other people to experience similar torments of jealousy. Eaten up by the insecurity of his condition, he cannot bear to see security in others, such as the patricians (e.g., Cassio) and the other upstarts (e.g., the Moor, who has risen above his lowly status by marrying the daughter of the senator Brabantio). Having first presented a rational Iago with a gen-uine affront to avenge, Shakespeare allows us to glimpse a more complex character; a victim of the monster that is jealousy who is contaminating others with this scourge.

For Iago, the end justifies the means and he revels in the cleverness with which he manipulates the naive and the credulous:

> The Moor is a free and open nature,
> That thinks men honest that but seem to be so,
> And will as tenderly be led by the nose
> As asses are. (I, 3)

His need for domination is the reflection of his own insecurity (saying of his rival Cassio):

> He hath a daily beauty in his life
> That makes me ugly. (V, 1)

Emilia, a pragmatist, is lucid without being corrupted by her knowledge; in love, but not blind; open to compromise, but upright. Despite the uncouthness of her husband (Iago), she obeys him. Despite her love for him, however, she confesses the truth after the murder of Desdemona, at the risk of her life. She is a sincere friend to Desdemona, but despite her loyalty she steals the handkerchief. She tries to teach Desdemona the benefits of situational ethics, of a degree of hypocrisy, and of coming to an arrange-ment with the powers above:

DESDEMONA: Would thou do such a deed [be unfaithful] for all the world?
EMILIA: Why, would not you?
DESDEMONA: No, by this heavenly light.
EMILIA: Nor I neither by this heavenly light
I might do't as well i'th' dark.

> **DESDEMONA**: Wouldst thou do such a deed for all the world?
> **EMILIA**: The world is a huge thing; it's a great price
> For a small vice (. . .). (IV, 3)

In short, Emilia is a modern moralist who reasons and a relativist who accepts reality, advocating compromise, but she remains true to certain values and ultimately sacrifices herself for them. She cannot prevent the dramatic events, but will contribute to justice (i.e., revenge) with respect to Othello and Iago.

Desdemona, the princess of innocence, moves over the course of the play from a victorious affirmation of her independence as regards social conventions (she marries Othello despite proprieties) to confusion (the world does not live up to her preconceptions) and resignation in the face of her tragic destiny. Living out her ideal without any concession to prudence, she is a plaything in the hands of Iago (who explains to her in Act II that a woman of high virtue is bound for a trivial destiny). She acts according to the requirements of her ideal and not those of reality (Othello's jealousy):

> And his unkindness may defeat my life,
> But never taint my love. (IV, 2)

She remains loyal despite everything, the incarnation of unconditional love – the only true love, all the others being mere economics. Innocence is not an unconditional virtue, and it could be argued that Desdemona has some responsibility for her destiny. More realism may perhaps have saved her, and Othello too; less holiness would not have overshadowed the other characters so much.

Innocence and virtue are public assets, in the sense that economists bestow on this term. The inconveniences resulting from the behavior of clever people are borne by everybody, but its advantages are largely appropriated by the selfsame clever people, while the benefits of innocence are usually – though not always – enjoyed by all and the costs are mainly borne by the innocents.

So, the judgments that we pass on leaders, as leaders, are different from the judgments we pass on them as human beings. Some admirable virtues can have appalling consequences for a community, while a sense of compromise and degree of cleverness redolent of a more circumstantial morality can sometimes prove more beneficial.[6]

---

[6] Koestler sums this up by saying that history is immoral: it pardons our faults, but not our mistakes.

Queries

2.1

A person who values and cultivates a private life of quality cannot excel as an organizational leader, and only a foolish society claims that leadership is consistent with a graceful and authentic private life. Leadership in organizations is no different from any other serious activity: It requires commitment, dedication, and a willingness to sacrifice almost everything else to a single-minded pursuit of excellence. It is no more reasonable to expect a great leader to be a "balanced" person with a "normal" private life than it is to expect such a thing of a great creative artist, athlete, or scientist. Ambition for preeminence is a jealous lover. It will not share and does not forgive dalliance.

Comment.

2.2

Many popular applications of decision theory and game theory to problems of leadership emphasize the cleverness of strategic maneuver and practiced deception in bargaining. In these treatments, the secret to success is found in misleading, outwitting, and out-thinking opponents.

Modern investigations in a game theoretic tradition have raised questions about such strategies, however. The issues are threefold:

1. Strategic cleverness often presumes that you are dealing with people who have substantially less intelligence than you do, a presumption that rarely is accurate.
2. Strategic cleverness undermines trust. As a result it precludes, or at least makes difficult, the long-term understandings and alliances that are necessary for long-term success in repeated games.
3. Strategic cleverness emphasizes the personal joys of being more clever than anyone else, thus challenges the personal self-worth

of others and makes them willing to sacrifice their own interests in order to deny you victory.

To what extent do such considerations pose problems for the
preachers of cleverness? What are the implications for training future
leaders?

2.3

Theories of organizational life often emphasize trust and loyalty along
with the complications of sustaining them. It is difficult to construct networks of collaboration and to maintain them against the
temptations of cleverness. Because incentives to revise agreements
unilaterally are frequently substantial, and the anticipation of such
defections makes partners wary of relying on each other, a first
principle of leadership is that if everyone is rational, no one can
be trusted. However, a second principle is that someone who never
trusts anyone will usually lose, because although no rational person
can be trusted, some people are innocent and can be trusted. Those
who, by chance or insight, trust those who can be trusted have
an advantage over those who are unconditionally untrusting. As a
result, a third principle is that anyone who is clever will try to look
innocent in order to be trusted by those people who might become
winners (by virtue of being willing to trust some people and being
lucky in their choice of people). But since the only reliable way of
appearing to be innocent is to be so in fact, a fourth principle of
leadership is that anyone who is genuinely clever will be genuinely
innocent.

Can any of this be untangled?

2.4

In Act I of Othello, the Duke, Brabantio, and Othello are concerned
with two primary questions: The first is whether Othello wrongfully seduced Desdemona. The second is whether such behavior, if
proved, makes him unacceptable as a commander of Venetian forces

against the Turks. Shakespeare acquits Othello of the first charge, thus making the second question moot.

What considerations are relevant to the second question? How do the characters in the play feel about them? To what extent do their feelings on the second issue affect their judgments on the first? To what extent are the arguments applicable to modern organizations and modern leaders?

2.5

In the moments immediately before and after Desdemona's death (Act V, Scene 2), Othello, Emilia, and Desdemona express their feelings about the justice of the death and responsibility for it. Their thoughts are found in outbursts, rather than thoughtful analyses, but it is clear that each of them has a different perspective:

- Othello believes that Desdemona was unfaithful, that her death was justified by her infidelity, and that he was responsible for her death.
- Emilia believes that Desdemona was faithful, that therefore her death was not justified, and that Othello was responsible for her death.
- Desdemona believes that her death was not justified, and that she herself was responsible for her own death.

A modern observer might well have questioned whether infidelity should be punishable by death, but that is not disputed among these three. The difference between Emilia and Othello turns on the fact of Desdemona's faithfulness and can be explained by Othello's gullibility in accepting Iago's scant evidence. On the other hand, the difference between Emilia and Desdemona is not a factual one but one of assigning responsibility and seems harder to explain.

When Emilia asks: "O, who hath done this deed?," Desdemona replies "Nobody; I myself." Develop an interpretation of that response. What is Desdemona's conception of responsibility? What are the implications for responsibility in modern organizations? For leadership?

2.6

In the final scene of *Othello*, Gratiano says: "All that's spoke is marred!" (VI, 2, 353).

How are we to interpret this comment? Consider in particular whether we should apply the comment only to what was said in this scene, more generally to the play as a whole, or even more generally to life? Consider also how the comment might be elaborated usefully. What are the issues? How does the play illuminate them? What are the implications for leadership?

CHAPTER 3

HERESY AND GENIUS: *SAINT JOAN*

Exploitation and Exploration

Finding the balance between exploration and exploitation is a major challenge for leaders.[1] We shall refresh our memories about certain observations that have already been made before discussing the leader's role in pursuit of this balance.

Exploitation is based on the efficient use of existing skills. It produces reliable results but runs the risk of sidelining more promising alternatives. Exploration consists of looking for new possibilities, at the risk of not looking at them closely enough to gain the full benefits of mastering them. The optimal mix between the two mainly depends on the stability of the environment and the time horizon.

In a situation marked by failure, exploration tends to find the way out, but in the short term it often leads to new failures, partly because most of the ideas that are explored turn out to be bad, and partly because the ones that could be good require a certain amount of practice. As at first sight they seem to be fruitless, other lines of research are pursued, instead of acquiring the skills that would make it possible to reap the benefits of previously identified possibilities.

The feeling of failure is obviously a subjective one and is reinforced by overambitious aspirations. It is also vulnerable to reinterpretations with

[1]   This theme has been extensively explored in March's research; see, for example: *Invitation à la lecture de James March*, p. 87; James G. March, *Three Lectures on Efficiency and Adaptiveness*. Helsinki: Svenska Handelshögskolan, 1994, and James G. March, *The Pursuit of Organizational Intelligence*. Oxford: Blackwell, 1999, chapters 7, 10, and 11.

hindsight: the person responsible for a decision will tend to interpret its consequences in a favorable light, whereas a changeover of power can lead to accusations that past strategies were failures. This explains the compulsive exploration in some fields (education, for example) where one reform is launched before there is time to evaluate the preceding one or to become competent in its procedures.

Conversely, an exploitation crowned with success tends to discourage exploration as the benefits of the latter are uncertain and remote in both time and space, while the experience gained through incremental adaptation of available expertise to new situations makes exploitation more and more efficient.

It is therefore very difficult to maintain a balance between efficiency and the capacity to adapt, as there is a tendency, in the case of success, to specialize and refine the procedures that have been successful; and, in the case of failure, to be impatient for positive results from novel innovations.

After a certain point, exploration is no longer profitable, as all lines of research have become exhausted (even though some of them were no doubt abandoned rather too hastily) and sufficient knowledge has been acquired to take advantage of discoveries made by other people. In general, it appears to be true that effective exploration requires knowledge, but not so much commitment to that knowledge that new ideas are rejected too rapidly. At the same time, the marginal yield of exploitation follows a downward curve. Exploitation refines and improves expertise, but refinement improves things less and less with time.

Can Leaders Selected for their Reliability Become Creative Leaders?

Leaders are selected by established institutions; they are, therefore, generally conservative and gifted with the talents required for exploitation. They are also expected, however, to introduce and oversee changes that may be needed. The stories of successful change recounted after the event by leaders, consultants, or researchers are deceptively simple, as they depict the leader as a hero guided by a vision that goes against prevailing ideas and is brought to fruition through heroic efforts. These stories, however, generally ignore the obvious problem that leaders face – when contemplating a large variety of deviant ideas, how is it possible to distinguish beforehand the ones that will be good from those that are merely deviant?

Most original ideas are bad ones. Those that are good, moreover, are only seen as such after a long learning period; they rarely are impressive when first tried out. As a result, an organization is likely to discourage both experimentation with deviant ideas and the people who come up with them, thereby depriving itself, in the name of efficient operation, of its main source of innovation. Even if the possible advantages of exploration are recognized, it is in the interest of an organization to have other investors (whether individuals or other organizations) bear the costs of experimentation if the benefits of successful ideas can be shared at no cost subsequently.

We also encounter this dilemma in the education of children. The ideas that a child finds original are rarely unique and rarely good. Teachers therefore discourage the emergence of these ideas, so that creativity only survives by accident, sometimes because the children are bad learners or because their environment "fails in its educational duties." The same is true of the education of future leaders, who are selected for their ability to solve known problems by using tried and tested methods.

In order to stimulate a sufficient level of exploration, we must understand the factors that determine either a taste for, or an aversion to, risk; in other words, what can make a decision maker opt for greater or lesser variability in results.

On an individual level, we know that:

- Danger can have positive effects (strategies risked "out of desperation" in a difficult situation). It can also have negative effects (paralysis when survival is threatened).
- Overabundant resources stimulate exploration (fewer controls, less fear of failure, institutionalized innovation).
- A person whose performance falls short of his or her aspirations will look for more variability than somebody who goes beyond them and whose main priority is to preserve what he or she has acquired.
- New resources will be invested in a more risky manner than resources that have been assimilated (and therefore integrated into aspirations).[2]
- A previous successful experience induces a superstitious belief in one's capacity to defy risks or to be lucky.

---

[2] When a resource is available for a sufficiently long period, we "count on it" and find it hard to do without it, but a sudden, unexpected addition is more likely to be exploited to the full (see, for example, Michèle Sebag, "L'argent du loto" (on money won at a lottery), MSc dissertation in economics, Universite Paris-IX, 1982).

On an organizational level, the uncertain and remote benefits of exploration have to be balanced against immediate, known costs. Organizations that favor risk taking tend to lack experience and to depart from the traditional, hierarchical model; in particular, they are likely to be decentralized with a relatively permissive system of central controls.

If creativity and the production of deviant ideas are to be stimulated, then bad ideas must be tolerated or even encouraged (for example, by congratulating students who make interesting mistakes). There could also be increased rewards for those whose deviant ideas turn out to be good. This is the function of patents and industrial property rights and, more generally, of all the systems that bestow substantial privileges and resources on those rare individuals who achieve success (as in sport, show business, and politics) in order to encourage other people to try their luck. Although one particular hare (who runs fast but sleeps too long) has every chance of being beaten by one particular tortoise, an army of hares in competition with an army of tortoises will almost certainly result in one of the hares crossing the finishing line first.[3] The choices of an organization therefore depend on the respective importance that it attaches to its mean performance (in which case it should recruit tortoises) and the achievement of a few dazzling successes (an army of hares, which is inefficient as a whole, but contains some outstanding individuals.[4]

It is also possible for organizational procedures unwittingly to affect participants' perceptions of their own success. Individuals who are frequently promoted because they have been successful will have confidence in their own abilities to beat the odds. Since in a selective, and therefore increasingly homogenous, management group the differences in performance that are observed are likely to be more often due to chance events than to any particular individual capacity, the confidence is likely to be misplaced.

[3] In a simple model, a tortoise advances with a constant speed of 1 mile/hour while a hare runs at 5 miles/hour, but in each given 5-minute period a hare has a 90 percent chance of sleeping rather than running. A tortoise will cover the mile of the test in one hour exactly and a hare will have only about an 11 percent chance of arriving faster (the probability that he will be awake for at least three of the 5-minute periods). If there is a race between one tortoise and one hare, the probability that the hare will win is only 0.11. However, if there are 100 tortoises and 100 hares in the race, the probability that at least one hare will arrive before any tortoise (and thus the race will be won by a hare) is $1 - (0.89)^{100}$, (or greater than 0.99999).

[4] In some situations, the potential winnings justify gambling on a large bunch of hares. This is what a venture capitalist does in a winner-takes-all market, in the absence of any reliable forecast about dominant future technology.

Thus, the process of selecting on performance results in exaggerated self-confidence and thereby exaggerated risk taking.

Furthermore, it is possible to play on individuals' irrational motivations for their actions: their duty to the State, their faith in a divine mission (Saint Joan) or in destiny (Kutuzov), their natural, uncorrupted instincts (the lower classes, according to Tolstoy, or the reflexes of a good soldier), or their obsessions (love for Desdemona, revenge for Iago, patriotism for the Irish rebels).

Geniuses are dangerous. Othello's instinctive action makes him commit an appalling crime, the fine sentiments of Pierre Bezukhov bring little comfort to the Russian peasants, and Don Quixote treats innocent people badly over and over again. A genius combines the characteristics that produce resounding failures (stubbornness, lack of discipline, ignorance), a few ingredients of success (elements of intelligence, a capacity to put mistakes behind him or her, unquenchable motivation), and exceptional good luck. Genius therefore only appears as a sub-product of a great tolerance for heresy and apparent craziness, which is often the result of particular circumstances (over-abundant resources, managerial ideology, promotional systems) rather than deliberate intention. "Intelligent" organizations will therefore try to create an environment that allows genius to flourish by accepting the risks of inefficiency or crushing failures . . . within the limits of the risks that they can afford to take.[5]

Diversity and Unity

We have seen that organizations have to achieve a delicate balance between exploration and exploitation, between geniuses and competent technicians, between the diversity that allows original viewpoints to emerge and the unity necessary for integration and coherent action.

In the literature on organizations, some authors focus on efficiency; i.e., the quest for unity in organizations depicted as coalitions of players with different viewpoints, objectives, and skills that have to be coordinated to achieve complex tasks. Others concentrate on the capacity for adaptation of organizations confronted by a changing environment. The terms of this debate closely resemble those we have already seen with reference to

[5] These are linked to the timescales of the decision makers. Are these shareholders of a family business concerned with long-term benefits, or financial directors who cannot allow the quarterly results to deteriorate on account of "chancy experiments?"

exploitation and exploration, but with the addition of symbolic connotations that are more politically loaded.

The renewal of an organization's members maintains its diversity while socialization promotes a certain unity. The norms of an organization and those of its individual members mutually adapt to each other. We can construct models[6] that demonstrate how an organization benefits, on the one hand, from having within it badly socialized individuals who test strategies that differ from the official one (the organization's "code") and, on the other, from perfecting this official strategy by drawing on some of the discoveries made by these deviant individuals.[7] In such models, the individuals who come out the best are the ones who learn quickly in a world where many learn slowly (to their personal detriment). Co-optation mechanisms make it possible to integrate into the command structure of the organization deviants who had been excluded from it but who have proved their worth.

We can object, however, that the way in which individuals must prove their worth to be co-opted into the dominant group often reduces their level of deviance, or accentuates the differentiation among the groups. As a general rule, politically weak, peripheral, or subordinated groups will advocate diversity and decentralization, while dominant groups will sing the praises of unity and centralization. Generally speaking, in any given hierarchical position, people tend to claim more autonomy (thereby demanding greater tolerance of diversity and decentralization from the central authorities of the organization to which they belong) and want to control anything dependent on them, thereby promoting a certain unity within their domain. Reciprocally, everybody must come to terms with the demands for diversity from their subordinates and the demands for coherence and unified procedures emanating from higher up the hierarchy.

The leader at the top of his or her organization symbolizes its unity and shared culture, while at the same time encouraging local diversity to a greater

---

[6] *Invitation à la lecture de James March*, p. 92, Scott R. Herriott, Daniel Levinthal, and James G. March, "Learning from experience in organizations," *American Economic Review*, 75 (1985) 298–302; and James G. March, "Exploration and exploitation in organizational learning," *Organization Science*, 2 (1991) 71–87.

[7] This fairly sophisticated model takes into account the fact that we do not know which of the deviant individuals' beliefs has made success possible. The organization will therefore adopt some of their rules, sometimes advisedly and sometimes out of superstition (the deviant crowned with success imposes his or her rule, but his or her success does not result from the application of this rule).

or lesser degree. It can be in his or her interest to minimize the tensions between the demands of unity and diversity by learning how to recognize, within the demand for diversity, those groups that will change their attitude as soon as they gain positions of leadership.

Saint Joan

George Bernard Shaw's *Saint Joan* is a "historical" play. Shaw did not pretend to reproduce real conversations, but his fictitious dialogues do recreate what he considered to be the essential structure of the story.[8] This freedom is perhaps legitimate if we consider that all history is conveyed by narrators of varying proximity to their sources, and that the distinction between real history and unabashed fiction is not as clear as it might seem.

The fact that Saint Joan is a young woman is important and does explain certain attitudes, or certain problems concerning the character's legitimacy, but, just like the race of Othello and the social origins of Iago, it is not the central theme of the play. The play is about the problem of genius. The genius is an outsider with respect to the institution, is badly socialized and therefore spells trouble, but has a deviant understanding of the world that ultimately turns out to be right.

Shaw's Joan seeks to impart her vision to others and to history. The other main characters in the play staunchly defend the interests of the institutions that they represent (the Church, the feudal lords, the Crown, the British, the army), perceiving Joan sometimes as a threat and sometimes as a possible instrument. The establishment first tries to thwart this genius, then allows itself to be swayed and adopts her, only to abandon her once the crisis has been overcome and the threat has disappeared.

Joan's visions and voices (which some people term inspiration, intuition, or the subconscious) are necessary for escaping an impasse, but incompatible with the paradigm they threaten. Their rational justification is constructed later on, in order to convince skeptics: "Well, I have to find reasons for you, because, you do not believe my voices. But the voices come first; and I find the reasons after: whatever you may choose to believe." (5)

---

[8]   As an Irishman writing in English, Bernard Shaw benefited from a greater distance and freedom in his treatment of an exotic character who was not a national hero to his immediate audience.

Anyway, Joan does not believe in a rational approach based on the quest for individual benefit:

> You do not understand, squire. Our soldiers are always beaten because they are fighting only to save their skins; and the shortest way to save your skin is to run away. Our knights are thinking only of the money they will make in ransoms: it is not kill or be killed with them, but pay or be paid. But I will teach them all to fight that the will of God may be done in France; and they will drive the poor goddams before them like sheep. (I,1)

Joan's victories are not, however, the triumph of heresy alone, and Joan's vision would be worthless without the experience and know-how of the experienced military commander, Dunois:

> No. No, my girl: if you delivered me from fear I should be a good knight for a story book, but a very bad commander of the army. Come let me begin to make a soldier of you" (2) . . . some day she will go ahead when she has only ten men to do the work of a hundred. And then she will find that God is on the side of the big battalions. (5)

As for Joan's miracles, the archbishop explains why they are perfectly legitimate:

> A miracle, my friend, is an event which creates faith. That is the purpose and the nature of miracles. They may seem very wonderful to the people who witness them, and very simple to those who perform them. That does not matter: if they confirm or create faith they are true miracles . . . When this girl picks out the Dauphin among these courtiers, it will not be a miracle for me, because I shall know how it has been done, and my faith will not be increased. But as for others, if they feel the thrill of the supernatural, and forget their sinful clay in a sudden sense of the glory of God, it will be a miracle and a blessed one. And you will find that the girl herself will be more affected than anyone else. She will forget how she really picked him out. So, perhaps, will you.

The genius confirms a truth, with as much intolerance as her contradictors, and she can trigger the required change when normal procedures lead to a dead end: "We want a few mad people now. See where the sane ones have landed us!" (Bertrand de Poulengy to Captain Robert de Beaudricourt, to convince him to throw in his lot with Joan.) So, heresy only overcomes intolerance when the institution is desperate.

The genius is abandoned by everybody, however, when her lucky star lets her down, and the heresy no longer brings success (cf. Anita Roddick, Steve Jobs, Margaret Thatcher, Bernard Tapie, Jean-Marie Messier):

> DUNOIS: And now tell me, all of you, which of you will lift a finger to save Joan once the English have got her? I speak first, for the army. The day after she has been dragged from her horse by a goddam or a Burgundian, and he is not struck dead: the day after she is locked in a dungeon, and the bars and bolts do not fly open at the touch of St. Peter angel: the day when the enemy finds out that she is vulnerable as I am and not a bit more invincible, she will not be worth a single soldier to us; and I will not risk that life, much as I cherish her as a companion-in-arms. (5)

The genius therefore makes it possible to explore unknown and sometimes profitable paths in a situation in which the exploitation of the run-of-the-mill skills mastered by the institution does not serve in a crisis. When exploration becomes too costly or creates too much uncertainty and threatens established positions, the institution abandons the genius. This scenario is repeated in the case of other providential heroes.

Queries

3.1

It is said that one of the most important lessons to be learned in a university is that you have to kiss a very large number of ugly frogs to find one that turns into a handsome prince or beautiful princess. In fact, most people at most universities have never witnessed even one transformation of this sort, and both the faculty and advanced students are inclined to discount the likelihood of such a thing ever happening.

In such a world, who will kiss ugly frogs? What are the implications for innovative organizational leadership?

3.2

Recent efforts to promote ethnic, gender, and national diversity in business firms have led both to legislation and to moral suasion intended to increase diversity in organizations. Advocates of such measures have emphasized the ethical and political imperatives of equity, the need to improve the social and economic position of ethnic minorities, women, and foreign nationals within corporations. Supporters of diversity augmentation have also often claimed practical competitive advantages to be reaped from diversity, arguing that ethnic, gender, and national variety makes firms better able to survive. Supporters of increased diversity have rarely been challenged on moral grounds (although specific programs sometimes have been), but their claims of increased efficiency are sometimes questioned:

1. The claim of competitive advantage is suspect in some quarters, being viewed as a fiction invented to make diversity programs somewhat more palatable in a pragmatic business world. The counter argument is that diversity necessarily reduces organizational coherence and unity, increasing coordination, control, and training costs.
2. A different criticism is that the benefits of diversity enhancement programs, though greater than their costs, are generally reaped by groups other than those who bear the costs. Thus, it is argued that the programs fail because those who gain from them are not in a position to implement them, and those who must implement them are unlikely to secure advantage from them.

What are the practical arguments in favor of diversity? What are the benefits? What are the costs? To what extent are the costs and benefits distributed differently? What are the implications?

3.3

Organizational leadership is a contradiction in terms. The essence of organization is routine, conventional behavior, bound by the standards of knowledge, morality, and legality of the time. The essence of leadership, on the other hand, is escaping the routine, the standard, and the contemporary to implement a new morality, knowledge and legality quite different from that seen by others. Leadership is pre-eminently anti-organizational. Leaders confront organizations rather than build or serve them.

Thus, to speak of the CEOs of business firms, the presidents of labor unions, the directors of governmental agencies, and the commanders of conventional military units as leaders is absurd. They are not and could not be. Leadership will always come from outside organizations and will always be resisted by individuals who are conventional and reliable enough to be given formal positions of authority. There is no possibility of an organizational career for anyone with true leadership capabilities and instincts.

Comment.

3.4

The Saint Joan of George Bernard Shaw's play is arguably a remarkably modern leader. She claims a vision and commitment to it, but her commitment is far from unconditional. It is based on the expectation that things will come out right. She is not a woman of faith but a woman deluded into thinking that if she pursues her vision in a single-minded way, God will protect her. She is more fool, than saint; and her elevation to sainthood is an affront to faith.

Modern leaders are, in a similar way, deluded into heroic commitments by the St. Catherines of modern life – journalists, pundits, and professors. The promises are the same – that heroic action will be rewarded by honor and respect – and those promises are as false as the ones made to Joan by her voices.

Yet, in a world dedicated to instrumental rationality, promises of success, happiness, and ennoblement may be the only way to elicit the personal involvement of talented people in the thanklessness of leadership. If we were honest with potential leaders about the likelihood of their being crucified, they would serve us with less energy and dedication. So, we lie to them and justify it, appropriately, by the service their foolishness provides to the larger good.

Comment both on the evaluation of Saint Joan and on the characterization of modern leadership.

3.5

Saint Joan is often portrayed as a story of the contradictions between naïveté and sophistication, between reality and illusion, between conventional wisdom and genius.

What is Shaw's conception of the relation between such opposites in human affairs? What is his resolution of the contradictions?

3.6

Shaw's argument is that genius is socially certified by history and cannot be predicted in advance. As a result, it is impossible to predict which ordinary heretics will become revered saints and which crazy crackpots will become scientific geniuses.

The argument is plausible, but it glosses over a possible distinction between saints and scientific geniuses. Some people would argue that whereas the creation of sainthood out of heresy is an arbitrary social construction sustained by shared beliefs but not otherwise validated, scientific discoveries have a basis in physical reality that cannot be arbitrarily enacted simply through shared belief.

Is the distinction valid? To what extent does it undermine Shaw's argument when applied to scientific genius? Are organizational leaders more like heretics/saints or crackpots/geniuses? What are the implications?

CHAPTER 4

AMBIGUITY, IRRELEVANCE, POWER, AND THE SOCIAL ORDER: *WAR AND PEACE*

Organizations, Ambiguity, and Incoherence

Organizations need coherence to facilitate communication, simplify control, and guarantee equity. They replace improvisation with procedures and loose agreements with rules and contracts. Coherence is, however, limited by the ambiguity of experience, by communication, and by the need to delegate. We often underestimate these ambiguities and their usefulness, and give more than its due to rational action aimed at achieving clear targets within a well-defined strategy. In fact, the targets that are pursued often appear vague, unclear, barely coherent, unstable, or endogenous – determined during the course of an action and often even by the results of this action. It is difficult to interpret events, to reconstruct what was really done, to identify the effects of actions, and to know whether the result should be dubbed a failure or a success. Problems, solutions, and actions are loosely connected, as are targets, the information used, decisions taken, and actions performed by different departments in the organization. Simultaneity is often the most decisive factor.[1]

---

[1]   These ideas have been developed, particularly in the garbage can model, see: *Invitation à la lecture de James March*, p. 42 and Michael D. Cohen, James G. March, and Johan P. Olsen, "A garbage can model of organizational choice," *Administrative Science Quarterly*, 17 (1972) 1–25. See also James G. March, *A Primer on Decision Making*. New York: Free Press, 1994, chapter 5.

This ambiguity in human perceptions and decisions can perhaps be illustrated by recurring themes in T. S. Eliot's poem *The Love Song of J. Alfred Prufrock*:[2]

> Time for you and time for me
> And time for a hundred indecisions,
> And for a hundred visions and revisions
> [...]
> In a minute there is time
> For decisions and revisions which a minute will reverse.
> [...]
> I have measured out my life with coffee spoons;
> [...]
> It is impossible to say just what I mean.

The discrepancy between the ambiguities of reality and our expectations for clarity in reality can provoke three types of reaction in leaders:

1. an attempt to make reality fit the discourse (Idealism);
2. an attempt to exploit the difference between the two (Realism); and
3. an attempt to make the discourse fit reality (Romanticism).[3]

Idealists (economists, political analysts, decision theorists, and business consultants) want to eliminate ambiguity by making organizations conform to their model of them. They believe in the possibility of making clear preferences explicit from the outset, of perfecting our techniques of observation and deduction in order to gain a better understanding of events, of improving decision outcomes via more precise analyses and a better control of their application, and of resorting to complex models if reality eludes

---

[2] This very long poem was read in its entirety during the course.

[3] This definition of Romanticism may be disconcerting. This attitude consists of appreciating the beauty of the world and humans as they are, embracing the richness of human contradictions and obscure, chaotic passions. In the same way, in a "behavioral theory of the firm," instead of starting from a normative model of a decision maker's rational behavior, March describes the behavior observed in organizations and seeks to understand to what extent it is intelligent and efficient; he therefore constructs a discourse based on observed (and assessed) reality and not the opposite. Corneille gives us lessons about the human condition, whereas Victor Hugo and Shakespeare show it with benevolence and indulgence.

simple descriptions. In the military sphere, for example, they believe that it is possible to define precise and logical rules of engagement (resulting in situations like the Bay of Pigs in 1961, the Cuban missile crisis in 1962, and the destruction of an Iranian airliner by an American naval ship in 1988).

Realists seek to manipulate ambiguity to their own advantage. They know how to sail against the wind by tacking and weaving their way between obstacles. Inside organizations they are persistent, overloading the decision-making system in order to divert their rivals toward other problems and proposing interpretations of history that serve their own interests. They know that it is often easier and more useful to influence the way in which the results of an action are perceived, the indicators analyzed by management, and individual reputations than it is to act on a reality that is in any case highly problematic. They therefore focus on the grooming of their own reputations, the content of reports, the measurement of indicators, and the mastery of sophisticated accountancy techniques.

Romantics revel in the charms of ambiguity. They love discovering the goal for their actions while they are performing them, thus participating in the emergence of a little bit of history and the construction of its significance. They believe that life is a poem, and beauty may be a better criterion than truth. As Adrienne Rich has written, "Poems are like dreams; you put into them what you don't know you know." Romantics willingly resort to the technology of foolishness,[4] treating their targets like hypotheses (which will be confirmed or otherwise), their intuition as a legitimate source of inspiration, hypocrisy as a necessary transition, reports and the need for consistency as a potential enemy, experience as just another theory among many. They live and act in a playful manner. A decision is an occasion for learning something about the goal they are pursuing; planning is a way of recounting history and interpreting the past. The art of a leader consists in evoking interesting meanings. Memoranda become a form of poetry and assessment reviews provide an opportunity to give shape to reality, like a sculptor molding clay. Board meetings are organized and experienced like theatrical performances.

---

[4] *Invitation à la lecture de James March*, p. 48 and "The technology of foolishness," *Civiløkonomen* (Copenhagen), 18(4) (1971) 4–12, reproduced in *Decisions and Organizations* and, in part, in "Model bias in social action," *Review of Educational Research*, 42 (1973) 413–29, reproduced in *The Pursuit of Organizational Intelligence*.

The Irrelevance of Human Intentions to History

War and Peace was written in the 1860s, just 50 years after the historical events that it depicts. The story it tells was still "close" to Tolstoy's readers, but not too close. The time of the writing was a time of social and political upheaval. Alexander II had reigned since 1856 and had implemented a cautious but liberal program. Before he was assassinated in 1881, he put a stop to the Crimean War, recalled the Decembrists, abolished serfdom, gave a certain degree of freedom to the press, reformed judicial institutions, and was about to give the country a constitution.

The novel is fairly loosely, not to say disconcertingly, structured, with numerous digressions that seem to be gratuitous to the development of both the plot and the main characters (who are anyway only identifiable some way into the book). It tells a story and discusses its significance, taking the viewpoint of God looking down on the world[5] and drawing morals from its events for the benefit of the reader. The novel has no central theme – or, better said, it has several – characters appear and disappear (Vaska Denisov, Platon Karataev), minor scenes are described in minute detail for no apparent reason (the wolf hunt, Natasha and her mother counting the towels, the departure from Moscow), events are sometimes disconnected from their cause, just as thoughts are from actions, and the novel does not really end (the epilogue could just as well be the introduction to a possible sequel).

The structure of the novel, or rather its absence, illustrates Tolstoy's view of history. We are plunged into a flood of events that nobody can immediately judge to be significant or not. Most of the trails that are opened lead nowhere. Things happen in a chaotic order and it is difficult to assess where they start and finish. In fact, well-ordered stories, like that of Rostov who, unable to tell the silly story of his fall from a horse as it really happened, tells the standard tale of a cavalry charge, are highly suspect. Stories are artificially ordered and simplified, using vague terms like "power," "destiny," or "genius." Tolstoy loves to juxtapose official history with an alternative version (for example, the plan for the Battle of Borodino and Napoleon's encounter with a Cossack prisoner, described by Thiers). Official history is a social construction, just like individual stories (e.g.,

---

[5] Although Tolstoy was particularly fond of philosophical digressions, the viewpoint of an omniscient narrator looking down ironically on the reactions of his characters is a characteristic of many classic novels (e.g., Balzac, Stendhal, and Hugo).

Natasha's story, the interpretations of the duel, and Pierre's marriage). Stories are altered to satisfy the expectations of their audiences and therefore seem credible: they confirm established truths, describe effects as being close to causes and proportional to them, and attribute an essential role to the action of leaders.

War and Peace develops Tolstoy's theory that history does not follow any defined structure, but arises from the complex interaction of count-less insignificant events. Battle plans cannot be put into practice as a host of unforeseen factors emerge and generals cannot be informed in time about what is happening on the ground. Kutuzov has fully understood this and makes do with pretending to have the situation under control in order to reassure his officers, without seeking to have any other influence on the course of the battle.[6] History bestows importance on some characters as the playthings of overwhelming forces, while forgetting about the minor ones. "What does tomorrow hold for us? Fate will decide between one hundred million possible destinies, depending on whether our soldiers or theirs run away or not, and whether such and such man is killed."

Furthermore, individuals have characters that are in constant flux, with fluctuating concerns, which present different aspects to different observers. Andrei, for example, is seen by the progressives as a liberal because he has emancipated his serfs and is cultured; conservatives see him mainly as the son of his father; women consider him an eligible bachelor; and some officers perceive him as a man of exceptional benevolence, while others find him cold and distant. They are all right – at least some of the time. Tolstoy shows us wise men who do not believe in widely acknowledged truths (Kutuzov and Karataev) and glorifies those who know how to live for the moment, like Natasha and Nikolai. He suggests, that although truth is accessible in rare moments, it is useless to search deliberately for it.

War and Peace presents us with people of an inconstant nature thrown into an inconsistent world. In particular, it focuses on three characters endowed by the society with position and wealth but confronted by adver-sity and irrelevance.[7]

---

[6] "The essential thing, when you are in command, is to take a decision, no matter what it is. You get frightened at first, but then with experience you realize that it all comes down to more or less the same thing . . . Whatever you decide," wrote Jean Anouilh in *The Lark*, his play about Joan of Arc.

[7] By "irrelevance" one means the absence of any possibility that an individual can act in a meaningful way, i.e., contribute with any guarantee of success to a transformation of that world in order to make it better or more acceptable.

Andrei Bolkonski is intelligent, given to introspection, aristocratic, even effete and is comfortable in a closely controlled world. He is cold and a little distant, distrusts emotions, and cannot tolerate vulgarity. He is not easily swayed by other people's opinion, though will not revolt against the social order despite being well aware of its limitations. He longs for a rational environment, does not like ambiguity, and in a way causes the downfall of Natasha by requiring her to make a considered commitment and wait a year to become engaged, thereby rejecting her spontaneity, carefree nature, and propensity to live for the moment. He is persevering, unobtrusively efficient, and scrupulous in fulfilling his obligations, while showing concern for the well-being and moral advancement of those who are dependent on him. In the face of adversity, he is courageous, but weakened by his need for rationality: he can only view Natasha and Anatole's affair through the prism of a rigid concept of honor, without feeling any deep need to take revenge on Anatole. He cannot bear the arbitrary and incomprehensible nature of the world. His intelligence gives him the lucidity to recognize the absurdity of war, the inflated self-importance of Napoleon, the stupidity of the salons in Saint Petersburg, the senility of his father, and the excessive religiosity of his sister, but it does not help him to make sense of his surroundings. His intellectual approach prevents his love for Natasha from carrying him away; in fact, he ends up destroying it, because he will not allow himself any mystical experiences (although he does get close on several occasions). He is not blind to the mediocrity of official heroes, but is unable to recognize real heroism when he stumbles across it (Tushkin). Andrei is a modern and well-educated character, conscious both of the need to act and of the impossibility of giving sense to his actions.

Pierre Bezukhov is clumsy, naïve, and romantic, his lack of social graces being particularly evident when he attends salons; he is spontaneous, often puerile (he dreams of killing Napoleon and is infatuated with numerology and Masonic mysticism), and easily influenced. His character is fully rounded. He avoids making decisions, gets married, fights a duel, and almost gets himself executed after a series of events that he does not understand and does not attempt to control. He is looking for a definitive and reassuring truth, with an enthusiasm that nothing can dampen. He ends up finding peace by immersing himself in everyday life. He is perhaps the most real character in the novel: he is neither distant nor "abstract" like Andrei and Tolstoy often describes his body or dwells on his eating habits. He refuses to take himself seriously, makes about-turns from one commitment to an other one, and throws himself into most undertakings with passion (his admiration for Napoleon, his carefree life, his marriage to Helene, his duel, his Masonic studies, his patriotism, his participation in the campaign and the Battle of Borodino, his plots to kill Napoleon, his communion with the lower classes): "We must live, love, and believe that we are here not only for today, on this acre of land, but that we have always been here and will always be here in everything." He never rebels against the gratuitousness and irrelevance of the world. He looks on passively at his betrothal with Helene, which has been arranged by other people. His walk on the battlefield at Borodino, oblivious to danger but totally point-less, illustrates the absence of any real meaning in the events unfurling around him.

Natasha Rostova is impulsive, full of confidence in life and in herself; she often flirts with disaster, but generally avoids it (except with Anatole Kuragin). Tolstoy describes Natasha without indulgence, although he cer-tainly appreciates her beauty and her exuberant approach to life. Her nature is passionate and highly narcissistic, although devoid of egoism: most of her attention is focused on herself, but she sincerely wants other people to be happy. She lives totally in the present, overflowing with life and sexual energy. Although she is not especially intelligent or virtuous, she gets every-thing she wants; her destiny is fulfilled. Her treatment, particularly when compared with the misfortunes of the virtuous Sonya, reveals a God indif-ferent to individual virtues, an unfair God who prefers people who are full of joy and life (or blesses with joy and liveliness the people he prefers). Adversity surprises her, but she fights bravely and effectively in crisis situ-ations, as when she organizes the departure from Moscow. She does not care about or even notice the irrelevance of the world, as, unlike Andrei and Pierre, she does not try to discover the significance of events.

The narrative prefers innocence to the sophistication of the salons, spon-taneity to reasoning; but these assessments are relative, and the characters are often presented as both admirable and contemptible, either sequentially or simultaneously, and virtue is not reliably well rewarded by life. People are faced with insoluble dilemmas, with their virtue being revealed through their efforts to be good rather than their capacity to discern good; they prove their value through the dignity with which they confront life, the cruelties of destiny, and the arbitrariness of divine favor. History is the result of a complex enmeshing of insignificant causes and realizes the plan of an elusive God. The ridiculous pretensions of Napoleon are contrasted with the resigned modesty of Kutuzov. The epilogue shows us Pierre, Nikolai

Rostov, and Natasha finally appreciating the charms of a simple, healthy life, but it also reveals the dreams of glory of the young Nikolai Bolkonski, Andrei's son, who is on the point of naïvely reliving the trials of his elders.

Neither Andrei, the cultured, competent rationalist, nor Pierre, the enthusiast running after the latest trends, nor Natasha, the adventurer always ready to plunge into action, is a hero. Andre, despite his uprightness and self-control, is limited by his cynicism and distant reserve; Pierre is open and always willing to learn, but he is a victim of his own passivity and ingenuousness; and, although Natasha benefits from her self-confidence and the dynamics of success, she is impulsive and narcissistic. Ultimately, however, they all achieve a certain amount of wisdom through experience, and give up fighting against the course of history. At a few special moments, some characters seem to be nearing an essential truth (for example, when Andrei is wounded, Pierre is in prison, Natasha is at the ball, and Nikolai is at the wolf hunt), but such moments of grace pass fleetingly. Life has prepared good leaders like Kutuzov to assume the responsibilities that are their lot, but this ability is not the result of any deliberate career plan; rather, it is dependent on their capacity to face up to the irrelevance of human action, whether by opposing it like Andrei, denying it like Pierre, or ignoring it like Natasha.

Irrelevance and the Anomalies of Leadership[8]

Identifying leaders who are more capable and deserving than the people under them is notoriously difficult. This problem arises when a leader is chosen by a rational agent like a board of directors and is further exacerbated when it comes to the politics of choosing a democratic political leader, for, as March and Olsen point out, the qualities required to win power are not exactly the same as those that are useful for exercising it.[9]

Two articles written by March, but barely touched on in his course – perhaps because they are based on fairly complicated mathematical

---

[8] This section has not been written from the original course notes, but from articles published elsewhere (J. C. March and J. G. March, "Performance sampling and social matches" *Administrative Science Quarterly*, 23 (1978) 434–53, and J. R. Harrison and J. G. March "Decision making and post-decision surprises, *Administrative Science Quarterly*, 29 (1984) 26–42), as well as an article by Thierry Weil "À quoi sert le chef : la modélisation subversive chez James March," in Eric Godelier (ed.), *Penser l'organisation*, Paris: Hermes, 2003.

[9] J. G. March and J. P. Olsen, *Democratic Governance*, Free Press, 1995.

models, while the course attracted students of widely varying mathematical competence – explain, first, why bosses selected after a demanding examination process often prove to be disappointments and, second, why bosses who have brilliant careers do not necessarily achieve more than other ones.

Why are we often disappointed by the performance of leaders selected on the basis of their past performance?

We are often disappointed by the performances of bosses. Is this just the result of the excessive promises they make before being chosen? Perfectly relevant psychological or sociological explanations are frequently put forward, but it is also possible to demonstrate that this disappointment is an inherent effect of the selection procedure.[10]

Let us imagine a recruitment situation in which we can observe the performance of candidates during the course of a selection test. We can add to the intrinsic performance, k_i, which is linked to the capacity of the ith candidate, an unknown quantity, ε_i, which is linked to whether the candidate is on good form at that particular time, whether the questions fall in his or her particular area of expertise, random error in the assessment tools, or to other specific circumstances. Let us suppose that ε_i is a draw from normal distribution with a mean of zero. The selectors, voters, or recruiters will observe the overall performance $(k_i + \varepsilon_i)$ of each individual candidate and choose the best one on the basis of this single, observable criterion, which is a combination of talent and luck. If the process chooses the maximum of $k_i + \varepsilon_i$ over a set of candidates, it tends to pick candidates who are either more talented or luckier or both. In a competition among many candidates who differ relatively little in talent, the differences in talent are likely to matter rather little compared with the differences in luck. In other words, a candidate has to be way ahead of the others to be sure of winning. And as the number of candidates increases, the role of luck also increases.

The corollary of this observation is that the performance of the chosen candidate will be disappointing more often than not, as the luck that helped him or her beat the other candidates cannot be counted on in the future.

[10] J. R. Harrison and J. G. March, "Decision making and post-decision surprises," *Administrative Science Quarterly*, 29 (1984) 26–42.

It is even possible to calculate, for a given distribution of "luck," the value of this "regression to the mean" (i.e., by how much the value of the candidate will probably be overestimated). This allows us to draw conclusions on the best selection methods for a given research budget, depending on whether we want to make sure we do not overlook an exceptional candidate (in which case interviews – however brief, i.e., leading to an imprecise ranking are conducted with a maximum number of candidates) or whether we want to be sure that the winning candidate does not fall below a certain threshold of competence (in which case a much more thorough examination is applied to fewer candidates, even if this means a reduced chance of discovering a genius). Selecting the winner of such a test, even when this involves a substantial random error, will still, on average, yield the best result. In general, however, the winner of such a competition will not be as good as is expected on the basis of the test.

Are bosses unusually gifted?[11] To what extent are people with brilliant careers in positions of great power more gifted than other people? In order to find an answer to this question in a particular case, March and March have studied the careers of superintendents (chief executive officers) of school districts in the American Midwestern state of Wisconsin on the basis of biographical data extending over a 33-year period.

The underlying model for the evolution of careers is based on the following somewhat plausible assumptions about the process of success and failure in administrative careers:

1.   If a superintendent performs satisfactorily, he or she will be retained in the post.
2.   If, after a certain time, a superintendent proves to have particularly bad results, he or she will be dismissed.
3.   If, after a certain time, a superintendent has obtained exceptionally good results, he or she will be promoted to a more important post.

The observation of a population of 1,528 individuals over 33 years in all the 454 school districts of the State of Wisconsin should allow us to distinguish three possible hypotheses to explain the superintendents' careers.

According to the first hypothesis, the superintendents are *capable to a greater or lesser degree*. The probability of resolving a crisis is proportional

---

[11]   J. C. March and J. G. March, "Performance sampling in social matches," *Administrative Science Quarterly*, 23 (1978) 434–53.

to their capability, which is considered stable in time. In other words, variations in performance are due to their innate gifts (and some – unsteady – chance).

According to the second hypothesis, the superintendents all have identical capabilities at the start of their career, but *they improve with every challenge they encounter*, with every crisis that they handle. In this hypothesis, acquired knowledge prevails over innate gifts, and excellence is considered as being linked with experience (but not with seniority, as crises occur at random, with some of the superintendents thereby benefiting from more *learning opportunities*). In the final hypothesis, all the superintendents have equivalent capabilities that are stable over time. They are potentially *equal and remain so.*

Over the period of observation, some of the superintendents enjoyed brilliant careers while others stagnated or were dismissed. Which of the three hypotheses is most compatible with the structure of the observed results? Curiously enough, any of the three hypotheses produces results that are totally compatible with the observed structure of the careers: the model does not allow us to select among them.

Thus, a process in which each individual is promoted according to his or her apparent merits can lead to great variations among individual careers, *even if all the individuals have absolutely identical capacities* and only owe their performance to the luck derived from being either exposed to, or sheltered from, apparent challenges. Within this rather large data set, it is not possible either to prove or to disprove that the ones who succeed have, on average, any greater innate or acquired capabilities.

One explanatory element is the fact that the candidates initially hired for their first post as a superintendent already form part of a selected population; the closer people are to the peak of their career, the more homogenous is the population, with any further selection depending on random "noise."[12]

We can draw three tentative conclusions from these data and this little model. First, one of the few ways of limiting the impact of selection errors

---

[12] "Noise" is a term used by physicists and statisticians to describe a random variation in something that they are observing, leading to a blurring of the measured "signal." So, the performance of a candidate in a selection test is the result of the superimposition of a signal (the part of the result that reveals the candidate's intrinsic capabilities) and noise (random fluctuations in the performance, perhaps due to the fact that the candidate is or is not on top form, whether the subject discussed is one he or she is familiar with, etc.).

(the statistical noise) is a prolongation of the observation period, i.e., waiting for a certain length of time before promoting managers who perform best or dismissing the ones who disappoint.[13]

Second, beware of heroes! Successful managers have increasing opportunity to demonstrate their capabilities, with more chance of benefiting from a fortunate combination of circumstances; the corollary to this, however, is their increased chance of disappointing later on (this point is similar to the above, but with the focus on subsequent events).

Third, managers will generally return poorer results in the posts to which they have been promoted than they did in their previous ones (luck does not operate systematically to their benefit). This will confirm the preconception that the new post is more difficult and demanding than the previous one, even if this is not actually the case.

Most people sitting in first-class seats in airplanes are therefore confident that their capabilities are superior to those of their peers, though the main reason for their rise up the ladder may often be just a series of lucky breaks.

If it is not possible to find a superior leader reliably via selection tests or an assessment of his or her success in the past, are there any specific factors that can be correlated with an individual's future, prestigious career? The search for such factors has been long. It has occasionally identified statistically significant factors. Most of those identified in a single study are not reliably replicated in other studies. Some of those identified (e.g., physical height) seem to be reliably significant statistically but not of a magnitude that is of practical significance. Perhaps the most reliable substantial factors – being born rich and being born male – are probably both too well known and too politically incorrect to note.

The Ambiguity of Power

Leadership suggests power, but power is a limited concept. Power is difficult to define and measure, and does not yield verifiable predictions. We can only affirm after the fact that the conqueror is more powerful than the conquered, which is of course a pure tautology. In short, the concept of power as a tangible and stable attribute in an individual is fairly useless. Nevertheless, it is a concept that is often used; the feeling of power is linked

---

[13]   If the results are not dependent on the leader's capacities, this precautionary luxury is obviously pointless, but changing the leader is just as futile.

to the esteem that people have for themselves (this is often a vicious circle, as a person's reputation for powerfulness or weakness contributes to his or her success or difficulties). Power gives rise to desire, envy, and celebration, but also to revulsion, fear, and jealousy. The democratic ideal demands that any possible disparities in power should be justified and, if necessary, limited. Power has an esthetic attraction (the image of a powerful man dominating nature or his enemies)[14] and it fascinates us.

A rough definition of power would be the capacity to obtain what one wants (or to help others obtain what they want). On an economic and *trading level*, power comes from controlling rare resources (precious bargaining chips) or having different preferences (coveting what nobody wants). On the level of *collective choice*, where a decision is some kind of weighted mean of the choices of the various participants, a person's capacity to obtain what he or she wants (power, according to the definition above) is linked to his or her weight in the decision-making process (power, according to some other definitions) and the congruence of his or her preferences with those of other people. An individual without influence will, nonetheless, manage easily to obtain the decision he or she prefers if his or her desires are correlated with the desires of the majority. Although everybody agrees that a person's "power" depends on the resources that he or she controls, the importance of preferences is all too often forgotten.

History can be seen as the continuous progress of Man's power over nature, but also as a permanent modification of the respective power of different groups and individuals in a no-win situation where only relative positions count. The taste for power can be considered an individual characteristic that varies from one person to the next, from one culture to another, from one sex to the other. Like the thirst for vengeance, ambition, or love, it is potentially insatiable:

> Other women cloy
> The appetite they feed, but she makes hungry
> Where the most she satisfies (Shakespeare, *Antony and Cleopatra*, II, 2)

Although power is unsatisfactory as a descriptive or explanatory concept, it nevertheless remains a central element in stories and their interpretations.

---

[14] Think of all the tales of battle that exalt the power of heroes, from the *Iliad* to westerns and other Hollywood films.

Hierarchical organizations are obviously systems for attributing power, justified by their effectiveness in coordinating individual actions, despite the presence of other possible forms of coordination, such as the market and non-hierarchical networks. They are systems regulated by social norms: if leaders wield their power to an excessive degree, they are considered tyrannical; if they are too self-effacing, they are considered weak. Leaders are therefore concerned about how they handle their reputation for power, as it is proof of both the efficiency of their organization and their own individual value. They are careful to act ostensibly as legitimate holders of power, to react ruthlessly against those who defy their authority, and to use public occasions to confirm their powers. In important respects, the staging and interpretation of the process matters more than any tangible result.

We evaluate the power of individuals by considering resources (hierarchical position and wealth), processes (e.g., who participates in what decision; behavior patterns, such as the degree of peremptoriness or deference with which opinions are expressed), results (who has obtained what he or she wants or imposed his or her opinion), and other people's attitudes (e.g., signs of respect or fearfulness). Each of these aspects can therefore contribute to a reputation for power, and a leader will seek to control more resources, organize the agenda for making decisions, manipulate preferences (his or her own and other people's), and encourage deferential attitudes in colleagues.

This may explain why the exercise of power is often ostentatious and ritualized, and why those without power can lack self-confidence and long for signs of recognition. The vexations inflicted by people who hold power sometimes serve to stabilize both their position and reputation. Power is, therefore, often not only destructive for those who do not have it, but also for those who do. It can corrupt their humanity and distort their feelings and relationships with others: exchanges of information are no longer innocent and apparent respect or affection becomes suspect. Power involves a loss of autonomy and freedom, as people who hold power depend on a complex web of alliances, are more exposed, and are subject to a stricter social control on account of their powerfulness.

People who do not exercise power may desire a strong leader and revel in the glory of belonging to a dominant organization or group (especially if rituals make it possible regularly to confirm this domination by humiliating rival organizations – for example, by depriving competitors of their market shares, beating the sports team of a neighboring country, or winning a war). They can also occasionally defy authority, especially if there is little risk and they have a chance to challenge the established hierarchical order. They can also try, without defying the established order, to manipulate the organization by bluff, acting as if they have more power or authority than they actually do. They can form alliances with the powerful, generally by exchanging a deference that establishes the status of the dominating party in return for substantial advantages, be this a large degree of genuine autonomy, self-interested rewards, or even power, whether hidden, real, or imaginary.

Even though power is difficult to measure and define, it plays a symbolic role that a leader cannot afford to neglect. He or she must understand the ambivalent feelings – part attraction, part revulsion – that it generates. Witness, for example, the fascination of the primal beauty of an army on the march or an efficient organization, or the exaltation of primal sentiments free from the constraints of ordinary civility in fights or shows of strength; and the condemnation of these by a society that aspires to a degree of equality and regulated relationships, the rage of fearful, humiliated weaklings, and the fear of strong individuals who dread losing their power (or having their personal relationships corrupted by their status) and are condemned to suspicion and to doing things that they do not want to do. Some people seek power, others fear it, others do both. Those who exercise it with the least difficulty know how to appreciate both its delights and its dangers and try to minimize the negative aspects by aiming to instill enthusiasm rather than fear and to rule with kindness and courtesy. Everybody recognizes people like this as leaders, which alone can be a source of resentment, so they must then learn to come to terms with the negative reactions that are inevitable despite their most benign intentions.

Can there be any fundamental change? Our deeply held beliefs about domination and subordination, hierarchy and the essential role of leaders make change difficult to imagine, particularly since they serve as stabilizing factors in a society. If there is to be change, we need to reconsider our ideas about an order founded on the domination of leaders and an endless tug-of-war among contending interests. We must be conscious of the merits of the current order – its efficiency, and its sometimes-perverse beauty (the elements of beauty found in war and violence, in the affirmation of power, in dependence and slavery, and in danger and humiliation, whether inflicted or suffered). We can nevertheless imagine a world that places less emphasis on the relationships of domination and seeks to achieve an efficiency similar to that of a hierarchical organization, while respecting the dignity of all its members, whatever their role.[15]

The Social Order

Leadership is embedded in a social system that defines a social order. The social order that Tolstoy describes in *War and Peace* differs from the one with which contemporary citizens of western democracies are acquainted, due to the importance of family ties in individual lives. The family is not a private domain, but the cornerstone of the social order with marriage being the means to confirm or improve one's position in terms of prestige and fortune. The importance of Pierre – a bastard with an ambiguous status – is radically modified, even in his own eyes, the day he receives his inheritance and becomes Count Bezukhov. The importance of the conversations in salons is derived more from the fact that they confirm the respective positions of the speakers than from their subject matter, just like most meetings and committees in organizations today. Tolstoy criticizes Russia for both the incompetence of its leaders – which partly results from selection based on family-related criteria – and the artificial lives of the urban aristocracy, as compared to the "authentic" values of the peasants and the countryside. This social order is rejected in the name of rationality by Pierre and Andrei, in the name of faith by Marya and Platon Karataev, for its pervasive incompetence by Dolokhov and Denisov, and for its restrictions on pleasure by Natasha. For all that, *War and Peace* is not a tract in support of rebellion. The characters who find Tolstoy's favor tend to be the ones who, while participating in the established system, develop a degree of personal independence from its more artificial aspects, but also know how to appreciate its occasional charms (the salons, the balls, the opera) with indulgence.

In *War and Peace*, the Russian social order based on aristocracy and family tradition is challenged both by a modern order founded on science and intelligence, as embodied by Pierre and Andrei, and by the appearance of new institutions, as represented by Denisov, Dolokhov, and Berg. The social order changes slowly, more slowly than the adaptation of individuals to it.

What is particularly striking about the social order and individual reactions to it, however, is the ambivalence of the novel. *War and Peace* exhibits,

---

[15] This theme is developed a bit further in Chapter 5.

on the one hand, Tolstoy's rejection of the artificiality of Russian high society, coupled with his admiration for the authentic peasant life close to the land, and, on the other hand, his empathy with the charms and beauty of the life that he condemns. Although the virtues that are extolled require escaping the tyranny of civilized artificialities, the book lovingly portrays the genuine attractions of vice, and suggests that virtue only makes complete sense to somebody who has experienced the pleasures of sin.

So, Natasha condemns what she discovers at the opera (V, 8), where she is "both scandalized and amused by the people present," but she is also seduced, realizes her own power of seduction, and finally allows herself to be manipulated by Helene and Anatole. *War and Peace* proclaims that most people cannot escape from the corruptions of society, but that it is possible to attain some degree of wisdom, based on a lack of faith both in accepted truths and in great expectations along with a capacity to lead a simple life and perform everyday tasks effectively. We can see here a resignation to a virtuous mediocrity, consistent with the destiny of Nikolai and Natasha at the end of the novel. They sacrifice the sometimes-artificial charms of life to the sobriety and wisdom of maturity. But the novel also presents, at the end, Andrei's son with the enthusiasms and energy to start a new cycle of hopes and disappointments.

Queries

4.1

Leaders are less important to the course of history than they are to our acceptance of it. They are inventions, but essential ones.

Comment.

4.2

Consider the following polemic:

> The first axiom of life in an organization is that you can have power
> or autonomy, but not both. The price of being powerful is giving up

freedom, for no social system can tolerate autonomous power. It is a lesson that is very hard to learn if you are new to power, for you imagine that power will make you free. It doesn't. Having power often feels good. It often allows you to affect the course of events around you, perhaps even make them better. But power is not a route to freedom. Power attracts power. It entangles you in a web of social attention and responsibility that robs you of independence. Most of all, it is inextricably linked to the pursuit of allies, and the pursuit of allies inexorably destroys autonomy.

What is the theory that underlies the polemic? How general does it purport to be? What parts of it are true, or might be true? What are the possible implications?

4.3

Consider the following questions posed by a student of modern life:

1. Why do children become more and more interesting as they age, and adults less and less interesting?
2. Why do communication theorists make poor conversationalists?
3. Why is it more enjoyable to be seduced by a poet than by an economist?

The answers to all three questions, we are told, hinge on differences in the attitude about preferences:

1. Children become more interesting as they age because they discover their preferences and construct themselves by acting. They act without good reasons and discover the reasons afterwards, thus changing and developing in an interesting way. Adults, on the other hand, act on the basis of known reasons and fixed preferences. They do not change even as the world around them does.
2. Communication theorists are poor conversationalists because they believe that objective of communication is to transfer ideas in such a way that the idea of the sender is received

without distortion. In a good conversation, on the other hand, the meaning of a communication is open, being transformed by a recipient into a more interesting message than was anticipated by the sender. Precision destroys conversation; misunderstandings enrich it.

3. Seduction by a poet is more enjoyable than seduction by an economist because, for an economist, seduction has a single, clearly defined objective. It involves selecting the optimal strategy for achieving that objective and moving directly to it. A poet does not distinguish between seduction and life. In neither is there a clear objective, but an openness to the charms and beauty of various processes and various outcomes.

Comment, drawing the possible implications for leadership.

4.4

Near the end of the account of the engagement at Schöngraben, Tolstoy reports Prince Andrei's feelings: "He felt distressed and sad. It was all so strange, so unlike what he had expected."

What distressed Andrei? Why was he sad, rather than angry? What are we to conclude about history from Tolstoy's interpretation of the events at Schöngraben? How does Tolstoy use the engagement to elaborate his ideas in later parts of the novel? What are the implications for leadership?

4.5

The opening scene of *War and Peace* takes us into the elegant and elaborate world of Petersburg and Moscow society typified by the salons of Anna Pavlovna and Helene Bezukhov. Tolstoy returns to the splendor, frivolity, falsity, indolence, and vanity of such scenes repeatedly in the novel.

Why? What is the point? How are we to react?

4.6

As he grew older, Andrei Bolkonski came to see the rituals of Russian social life as false, the claims of generals as ridiculous, the dreams of lovers as self-defeating, the hopes of social reformers as naïve, and desires for personal fulfillment through commitment and action as fruitless. Similarly, many aging commentators on modern life see plans for world peace as foolish, ambitions for a healthy environment as pie-in-the-sky, "safe sex" as a contradiction, efforts to produce ethical behavior in the market place as silly, and desires for personal self-discovery through active engagement in the pursuit of ideals as childish.

Why might we find disillusion about the possibilities for effective action to be correlated with age and experience? What are the possible implications for leadership?

CHAPTER 5

GENDER, SEX, AND LEADERSHIP[1,2]

The Gender of Leadership in Organizations

With a few rare exceptions (such as eighteenth-century Russia, where the throne was most often occupied by a woman), men are over-represented in positions of responsibility, although recently we have seen a modest rebalancing (Margaret Thatcher, Cory Aquino, etc.).

[1] When March discussed the relationships between leadership and both gender and sexuality, he pointed out that research indicates that students in university lectures generally thought more about matters connected with sex than about the topics of the lectures. He wanted them to note that for once the topic in hand had perhaps coincided with the concerns of his audience!

[2] Issues connected with the role of gender and sex create a minefield of ideological and emotional complications that render research difficult and its results difficult to interpret. March admits that his apprehension about these issues is heavily influenced by the fact that he is a man, born and bred as such and rather happy to be so, even though he thinks there is no particular merit in belonging to the male sex. His fundamental belief is in men and women as human beings, and he finds it inconceivable that a just society can make gender a subject of discrimination – especially as regards opportunities for personal growth and participation in parental functions or professional success. He further believes the current situation of male economic and organizational superiority and female moral and ideological supremacy to be neither stable nor desirable. This does not prevent him, however, from distrusting the simple solutions bandied about in some quarters. Any significant progress would require, at one and the same time, new approaches to the organization of both the family and the professional environment, as well as a sea change in our received ideas about the roles of power and hierarchy and our depictions of sex and sexuality. At the moment, all these matters are closely entangled, but these difficulties, and the fact that it is an emotionally loaded subject, should not prevent us from entering into respectful and rational discussion of these issues.

The norms for organization are therefore dominated by male values, which are, of course, constantly evolving. Numerous psychological experiments and sociological observations show how manhood is attained by defying authority and fighting for power against other men, in physical combat or its symbolic equivalent:

- Men opt more willingly than women for strategies of competition and confrontation.
- Men, unlike women, are stimulated by a competitive situation.
- Men have more conflicts with authority than women (school, criminality, prison population, etc.).
- Boys have more experience of setbacks followed by a struggle for success.
- Boys have more aggressive games and behavior.
- One can see aggression toward newcomers in a group of boys and a greater aggression on the part of newcomers who have to assert themselves in a group.
- A man must hide his feelings and emotions ("real men don't cry").

Organizations present all the characteristics of male gangs, although physical violence is forbidden, being replaced by verbal and economic competition and professional rivalry for promotion. Women often reinforce this situation by judging men in accordance with the status they acquire in competition with other men. A man's status is determined by his position with respect to other men; his position of power with respect to women is generally not an important issue, possibly because it is assumed but also possibly because it is not relevant to male status orders.

The difficulties experienced by women in organizations are those of every minority group whose culture is foreign to the local norms. Men are often unaware of their own norms and are therefore insensitive to the problems that they pose for women. As the latter have less power or facility for defying the established authorities, they adopt the behavior of submission, bluff, or alliance with minority or fringe groups.

Romantic novels, generally written by women for women (including a sprinkling of distinguished writers like Emily Brontë, Virginia Woolf, and Doris Lessing), present an interesting theory on women's expectations. Typically, a meeting between a man and a woman leads to disappointment; the man is cold, hostile, and overbearing; they separate and the man realizes that he is in love with the woman; she reinterprets his coldness as a sign of love; he convinces her that he loves her and they end up being reunited. The woman is intelligent and independent, a fighter, while the man is strong and kind; the hero can be aggressive if it is for love or if his aggression is directed toward the outside world, but in no circumstances can he be timorous; the heroine gets what she wants, but the man retains his dignity. The heroine is afraid of being bullied, but also of being abandoned; she is reassured by a powerful but sensitive male character. In short, these novels describe women's search for autonomy and fulfillment in a world where they have little direct power: they refuse to be dominated (they can even get their chosen man to go down on his knees for them). Rather than having to choose between a tyrant and a wimp, they imagine a man who is dominant and powerful in the world of men, but submissive to their desires (strong, but kind; virile, but attentive; protective, but tender, etc.)

While men are better prepared by their education for competitive strategies, women are better prepared for liaison strategies. One such strategy minimizes the importance of power games in relationships with bosses. It should be noted that the relationship of a boss with subordinates is by its very nature polygamous (unlike the relationship of subordinates with their boss) and it involves the boss exchanging substance for marks of deference. This polygamy can contribute to a social reprimand for the sexual elements entailed in this relationship.

Women's less-dominating management style is often described deprecatingly within a male culture (Cory Aquino, for example, was criticized for her "indecision"). Schematically, the differences in style are usually described in approximately the terms shown in Table 5.1.

Some of the female characteristics are linked to low status and are shared by men in situations of weakness, while women in positions of strength

Table 5.1 Differences in style between men and women

Men	Women
Hierarchy	Connections and deference
Division of work	Personal relationships
Instrumental rationality	Contextual reasoning
Clear demarcation of territory	Subtle boundaries
Domination of the group	Bonding language and action

often have a style that is considered masculine. Others are more closely linked with sexual identity – women in positions of strength retain female characteristics while men in subordinate positions still have a male attitude.

Delegation and mutual trust, linked to an understanding of the process as a whole, make it possible for all individuals to accomplish their own tasks while taking into account the constraints of other members of the organization. Mutual trust is based on a shared understanding of, and identification with, organizational goals among individuals proud of their organization and satisfied with the symbolic recognition they receive from it.

Unobtrusive coordination involves everyone being informed of the overall situation, being trained to react appropriately in any given circumstance, and having confidence to take on-the-spot initiatives. It involves tolerance of mistakes, to avoid discouraging useful experimentation at a local level. Widely diffused competence and initiative, allied with coordination via mutual adjustments, allows for efficient reactions and avoids the need for costly specialists or hierarchical controls.[3] Heroic leadership is neither required nor helpful. The emphasis on the density of organizational competence is an echo of that highly respected captain of industry, Alfred P. Sloan. His management procedures were designed to ensure that General Motors depended, not on a few miraculous figures, but on the functioning of competent and committed heads of divisions.

The qualities required to coordinate organizations unobtrusively, while promoting mutual trust and individual recognition for all, seem more "feminine"[4] than the ones currently associated with a heroic leader.

Is this sexist pattern of leadership styles likely to change? It is possible that the strategies of the weak are more profitable to the group as a whole than the behavior of dominant individuals. It is frustrating for countless women, almost certainly disadvantageous for society as a whole, and morally disagreeable. Once again, we can have an idealistic, realistic, or

---

[3] These mundane elements of leadership are discussed in Appendix 2. This section has not been written from March's course notes but from articles published elsewhere ("Heroic leaders and prosaic organizations," lecture by James March in Mexico in 1988, which appeared in French in *Gérer et Comprendre*, June 2000), as well as being adapted from Weil's articles "Les mythes du management et les organisations floues," Colloque "James March ou l'itinéraire d'un esprit libre," Poitiers, October 17, 2001, *Revue française de gestion* 28 (139, July 2002) 187–94, and "À quoi sert le chef : la modélisation subversive chez James March", in Eric Godelier (ed.), *Penser l'organisation*, Paris: Hermes, 2003.

[4] In other words, these qualities are the ones that are currently associated with the management style of women in positions of power, such as those outlined schematically in Table 5.1.

romantic attitude. The idealist has a nostalgic enthusiasm for the traditional order and seeks to replicate as precisely as possible, extolling the charms
of boy gangs, hierarchy, specialization of the sexes, and competition for
power. *War and Peace* bears witness to the attractions of this old order,
even while rejecting it.

The realist seeks to equip women better for the current rules of competition, by means of a "bilingual" education that allows them to master
male codes, while dealing with social structures that are (albeit indirectly)
harmful to women's professional careers (for example, the obligation
imposed on candidates for business schools to have had significant professional experience can penalize young mothers).

Finally, the romantic tries to transform existing practices, in particular
by asserting the usefulness of female styles of leadership for organization:
a better grasp of context; a tolerance of complexity, ambiguity, and incoher-
ence; a more empathetic and less authoritarian style in leadership; and flexible cooperation strategies rather than open competition. In the absence
of any change in approach that forces a rupture from schemes describing
the world in terms of power and domination, the women who now find
themselves co-opted into a system whose norms remain male ones become
frustrated as they have to sacrifice certain aspects of their femininity. Nevertheless, they constitute the Trojan Horse of change and their bilingualism
often allows them to take more effective advantage of opportunities that
escape their male colleagues. The world is changing, but our official ideology runs ahead of the real functioning of our organizations. Or maybe this
hypocrisy is, as so often, a means for introducing a real transformation.[5]

Sexuality, Organizations, and Leadership

Sexuality is present in many forms in organizations. Leaving aside overtly
sexual acts themselves, organizational functioning feeds on a range of sexual

---

[5] March has developed elsewhere, in a "technology of foolishness," the idea that hypocrisy
could constitute a necessary transition between vice and virtue. An unscrupulous schemer
who declares himself to be good is maybe in the process of exploring an attitude that is new
to him, and the satisfactions that he finds therein will make any potential conversion easier
to undertake. (See "The technology of foolishness," *Civiløkonomen* (Copenhagen) 18 (4) (1971)
4–12, reproduced in *Decisions and Organizations* and partly included in "Model bias in social
action," *Review of Educational Research* 42 (1973) 413–29, and reproduced in *The Pursuit of
Organizational Intelligence*, Oxford: Blackwell Publishers, 1998).

attitudes, imaginations, and interpretations that affect everyday life. Organizations take pains to punish unacceptable acts of sexual aggression and harassment, but students of organizations and leadership tend to ignore other aspects of sexuality.

Private fantasies and the social control of behavior

It has been said that the primary sexual organ is the brain, presumably because imagination plays an essential role in sexuality. The imaginative world of sex provides a means of escape from real life that can be considered pernicious or overly intrusive – if, for example, a sex object is someone who produces an orgasm in somebody else's sleep, it could be asked by what right a person is authorized to invite another person into his or her dreams. The imaginative world of sex is nevertheless a source of pleasure that enriches life, energy, creativity, and joy.

The expression and depiction of sexuality follow social and ideological norms that are constraining but also in constant evolution (and, like teenage slang, always incomprehensible to the preceding generation). Terms such as "rape" or "sexual aggression," which are highly charged emotionally, now embrace behavior that would not previously have been defined as such. This has an ambiguous effect, as it extends the opprobrium evoked by these terms but trivializes the horror associated with them in their previous use. Another example is the term "sensitive lover," which traditionally meant a lover who is attentive to a partner's needs and desires and concerned about adapting his or her behavior to these needs, but nowadays tends to denote a man or woman who acts and talks in a stereotyped manner to show that he or she is adapting to the supposed generic desires of the opposite sex; i.e., somebody with no sensitivity toward the specific needs of a particular partner. The sensitivity is displayed rather than applied in practice, for it has become an ideological token and a cynical response to social demand.

Organizations offer a natural setting for the expression and structuring of sexuality, if only because people spend a lot of time in them and find numerous opportunities to meet other people and interact with them in depth. In this context, however, men and women differ in their expression of sexuality; men talk about sex more and are more inclined to demonstrate their heterosexuality.

Social norms provide a framework for sexuality in organizations. The effects of sexual impulses can either be unsettling for the normative order, or supportive of normative integration. Insofar as sexual displays or behavior appear to be potential threats to the social order, they are likely to be repressed. Reciprocally, insofar as organizational authorities repress sexual actions or attitudes, displaying them overtly may be a way to defy authority in the name of freedom, deviant subcultures, or age cohorts. The social attitudes involved veer between contradictory emotions:

- *Fascination*, a pathology linked to the development of the social and behavioral sciences, to contemporary society generally, or a particular society;
- *Repulsion* in the face of an addiction considered an affront to hygiene (in the same way, for example, as tobacco) or good taste (as Lord Chesterfield put it, "the pleasure is momentary, the position ridiculous, and the expense damnable"); and
- *Enthusiasm*, for sexuality as a manifestation of life and joy.

The peculiar result in American society, a political democracy infused with religious fundamentalism, is a traditional combination of liberty and prudery.[6] It juxtaposes a glorification of fine sentiments and formal respect for individual freedom, counterbalanced by a social vigilance that seeks to punish sinners. All this leads to a somewhat hypocritical attitude as regards sin, which is the subject of public condemnation and private enthusiasm. In American culture, therefore, recognizing sexuality or enjoying sex means risking disappointment, disapproval from other people, and self-disgust.

Organizations are, at one and the same time, embedded in society and protected from its regulatory pressure by their members' willingness to respect and enforce specific organizational codes that partly replace the rules of society as a whole. As organizations are structured in terms of hierarchy and power relationships, the aspects of sexuality linked to power play a prominent role. Men who hold power become sexually attractive and sexual exchanges confirm their power.

[6] France, on the other hand, as Sylviane Agacinski has observed in her "Politics of the Sexes", abhors Puritanism: "Relationships between women and men have always occupied an important position and the sex trade itself is fairly free. In a way, we apply the principle of laicism to our sexual and amorous life: sexual matters, like religious ones, are strictly private. . . . Public opinion itself separates, more easily than elsewhere, the judgment that it passes on public figures for their talent or competence, in whatever field, from any considerations about their choices in their private life, particularly sexual ones. . . . It is unimaginable here that an individual's personal habits can destroy his or her career (as is the case, in other countries, with marital infidelity or homosexuality)."

Sexual harassment

Our heightened sensitivity to the problem of sexual harassment has reduced its frequency, but has made it more visible. This is a characteristic of all criminal behavior that is exposed to public scrutiny: we see both a drop in the number of objectively verified cases and an increase in the number of cases that are denounced. Society's attention is aroused by an epidemic of reprehensible behavior, but this also gives rise to publicity that insidiously leads to other reprehensible behavior.

Organizations are exposed to this problem due to the importance of hierarchical position in the control of resources, to men's dominant power, and to the central role of sex as a motivation or as a resource. Harassment is an expression of domination of the weak by the strong. It thus fits into a mode of operation that is routine in organizations, where the strong routinely humiliate the weak in accordance with patterns inculcated by masculine norms, but it extends these patterns of domination into an area that is usually protected by social restrictions. Sex is indeed a culturally sensitive area and sexual exchange is not viewed in the same way as other types of exchange. It falls within the domain of the private and personal, and so slips out of the grasp of an organization. Contemporary standards of acceptable and decent behavior condemn harassment unequivocally, but the traditional patterns of women's education and socialization lead many of them to adjust to a reality, however unpleasant, that they feel cannot be avoided. In a male world where sexual prowess is a sign of power and sexual domination a prerogative of power, the real issue is more often power than sexuality.

To counter the problem of harassment, legal and regulatory protective measures have been implemented; in universities, for example, the rules on acceptable behavior in relations between teachers and students seek to protect women from the pressure of men. Of course, as we have learned to pay attention to the vulnerability of potential victims to intimidation and humiliation, we have also learned simultaneously to attend to the vulnerability of the accused, for behavior can be redefined later on and an accusation can give rise to social penalties almost as serious as those associated with proven guilt.

Although there is little question about many acts of sexual harassment, it is not easy to define the exact boundaries. One position is the extreme, whereby everything that can be construed as harassment is harassment. Such a criterion instills prudence in a potential harasser, but its legal basis is dubious. It is as if we were to say that everything that is perceived as unjust is unjust. A more balanced position consists in allowing "reasonable" people to use their common sense to decide what constitutes an act of harassment. This is the tradition of many judicial systems and it has some merit, despite its ambiguities. It is more difficult to put into practice, however, when sub-groups in a society – in this case, men and women – have cultures that are too different to be able to agree on what is "reasonable." This leads us to the more formalist position, which consists in wanting prescriptively to define a closed list of reprehensible actions – but this creates a very rigid assessment framework in a field where ambiguous elements are numerous and the context is crucial. There would be a risk of condemning practices that are admitted in many contexts (such as giving somebody a kiss), while exonerating more pernicious behavior.

Sexual relationships

Ordinary sexual relationships are distinguished from harassment by their bilateral consensual nature; i.e., they involve mutual consent. The very concept of consent is, however, fraught with ambiguity, as is well known from discussions of "informed consent" in medicine and law. The subtlety of the process of seduction only intensifies this ambiguity. The idea of consent supposes that the people in question clearly know what they want, but their desires may often be hazy, changing, and affected by circumstances. The problem becomes even more complicated when consent is considered retrospectively, sometimes many years after the actual events. Memory is often affected by an individual's mood at the moment he or she tries to remember his or her frame of mind at the time of a past event, and is clearly biased by retroactive rationalization. This already hazy issue of consent becomes murkier still in cases of less socially legitimate relationships, such as homosexual relationships in organizations where the norms are traditionally heterosexual.

A liberal society is generally intolerant of restrictions imposed on freely consented exchanges, which are considered the basis of a free life in society and a way of allowing everybody to improve his or her situation. However, the very nature of exchange makes the idea of "consent" difficult. What exchange is not constrained to some extent? Who would not prefer to keep what he or she is giving if possible, even if he or she gives it up for something he or she covets even more? If exchange is a legitimate basis of social relations, how can we condemn self-interested exchanges of friendship or sexual favors? The latter represent a resource that is particularly important to somebody who does not have many others. The exchange of sexual favors for economic favors is one of the bedrocks of traditional marriage in a world in which women have few other routes of access to economic resources. Love obviously goes beyond this concept of exchange, indeed denies it; but marriage as a socially managed relationship is normally constrained to keep husband and wife in a reasonably balanced exchange relationship. Similarly, the exchange of sexual favors for organizational favors is common, and their traditional positions mean that it is generally women who grant sexual favors to men who control the organization's resources.

These exchanges constitute a problem for people who lack resources (men without power and women without allure); those who have other resources to achieve their aims (seductive men who attract women anyway, or competent women who earn favors from the organization by virtue of their organizational talents); and, finally, those who condemn these exchanges of favors on moral grounds. This moral opprobrium finds the idea of sexual relationships based on exchange as intrinsically degrading, arguing that the value of sexual intimacy is partly derived from its independence from the sphere of financial exchanges. (In a different field, some voluntary blood donors stopped giving blood as soon as they were offered financial remuneration.)

It is also possible to invoke an inalienable right, whereby we are guardians or proxies, but not owners, of certain bequests, such as political rights, children, responsibilities within an organization, morality, and, maybe, sexual choices. Trading something under our guardianship, something for which we are accountable (organizational resources, as well as our sexual integrity) is therefore a form of corruption.

All these considerations legitimize the control of sexual relationships within organizations, even those apparently involving consent, in the same way as the use of an organization's resources is regulated to avoid corruption and extortion, or certain types of hazing or ragging are forbidden to protect personal dignity from humiliating practices. This regulation is enforced by the law, but also by social pressure and conscience.

Ambiguous sexual behavior

The significance of a particular behavior is affected by modes of expression, which vary from one culture to the next, and our interpretative

framework, which evolves over the course of time. We can therefore understand with experience that something that we once considered an oppression inflicted by our teachers or bosses was in fact appropriate professional
behavior. We can discover the charm of things that previously seemed to
lack interest, like ballet or accountancy. With the benefit of distance and
experience, the harsh punishment meted out by our parents may seem to
have been an act of love, flirting with a colleague may seem to have been
sexual harassment, and our behavior over the course of a drunken evening
may seem to have been shameful and humiliating.

All these problems are intertwined in the field of sexuality, especially
when some things are important in one culture, but a matter of indifference in another. Everything runs more smoothly when individuals with
more power are particularly attentive to the problems and feelings of those
with the less power. Generally, therefore, in most organizational situations,
the inequalities of power impose greater obligations for sensitivity on men
than they do on women.

The reinterpretation of the past adds a further difficulty. Worthy and
decent behavior normally consists of caring about other people's reactions
and being on the alert for signs of uneasiness or suffering, but this becomes
impossible when suffering appears later, as people change their assessments
of things that they once accepted, even encouraged. Retrospective interpretations evolve to serve needs for esteem, ambitions, or desires for revenge;
and anticipating them currently often seems to be an invitation to total
immobilization.

The sexuality of leaders

Male leaders must take these difficulties into account. They cannot expect
to live in an "authentic" environment, as the attitudes, feelings, and recept-
ivity of the people with whom they deal are substantially affected by their
position of power. In the sexual domain, power is an aphrodisiac; but the
sexual attractiveness of leaders wanes (both in reality and in memory) when
power wanes.

The aphrodisiac effect of power arises from the fact that the trivial financial aspects of the exchange of protection for sexual favors have been very
subtly integrated into our social and psychological norms concerning sexuality, so that a man's sexual pleasure is often linked to an acknowledge-
ment of his power by his female partner and a protective attitude towards

her. This recalls our earlier discussion of female fantasies about a strong, protective man in romantic novels. In a male world, sexual competition provides one reason for pursuing power, derived from women's attitude to power. A man's sexual standing basically depends on how much he attracts the women who attract him. Power does not offer the same sexual benefits for women as for men, which partly explains why men seek it more and why women exercise it better – they do not associate the experience of power so much with the joys, pleasures, and tribulations of sex.

What happens when the leader is a woman? It could be argued that the fact that women can now gain power more easily by their own merits will make strategies based on sexual liaisons less useful – as well as more demeaning for those women who do resort to them – and it will reduce the sexual attraction that power confers on leaders. So, the success of professional women may mean a loss of sexual potential for male leaders, not because they are competing against each other, but because they lose part of their power of attraction, at least with respect to women in positions of power.

The fact that boys spend a long time under the authority of women – their mothers and their females teachers – makes conjectures about male discomfort with female authority complicated. Typically, they have lifetimes of experience being subordinated to women in formal situations without thereby losing status among other males and thus without losing sexual attractiveness. It is possible that the reticence shown by some men who find themselves working under a woman reflects resentment at being in a lower position, rather than having much to do with the gender of their boss.

The exercise of power does also make some women more sexually attractive and they occasionally both flaunt their sexuality and exploit their control over resources to secure male partners. The mechanism of sexual attractiveness is different from that among men. Where men compete with other men for male dominance in order to secure female partners, the dominance position of women among women has no obvious role in determining female attractiveness to men. Any speculations about the sexual attractiveness of powerful women to men should probably be left for conversations over wine, but perhaps it stems from the extent to which dominant men find them an interesting challenge.

The relationship between leadership and sexuality poses numerous problems. It upsets criteria of a rational society based on merit, as well as relationships among people. It complicates the functioning of organizations, whether through inappropriate confusion between professional and personal domains of life, the implications of sexual relationships at work for family harmony, the dangers of harassment or accusations of harassment, unbalanced relationships, or attitudes that differ according to gender. Furthermore, the infantile or adolescent nature of male sexuality, bogged down in a fight for domination with other males, leads to behavior reminiscent of young roosters, more intent on striking advantageous poses than on achieving results. Confrontation can easily escalate into violence or war. Taboos such as incest can be seen as the last line of defense against the element of disorder that a free sexuality threatens for society and family organizations.

It should be noted, finally, that the problems are less the inevitable consequences of sexuality itself than of limited views of both leadership and sexuality. Among other things, for example, sexuality extends beyond heterosexuality to embrace a variety of other forms. A more open vision considers leadership to be linked to a wide range of motivations and possibilities, sees sexuality as a fundamental dynamic force, unconnected to any exclusive, or even specific, relationship. We must ultimately accept that in the field of sexuality, as in so many others, risks are inevitable characteristics of human existence and important aspects of freedom.

Sex is not the only thing in life, but many aspects of life are enriched by an awareness of the sexual elements they contain. Sexuality comprises a major source of energy and beauty. As more women occupy positions of power, so they will increasingly develop many kinds of sexual nuances and gratifications connected to leadership without confining themselves to the ones already developed by men. It is undoubtedly naïve and romantic to imagine that a world enriched in this way will be more interesting and exciting, and it seems likely that many people will pine for the simplicity of the old order.

Queries

5.1

Some of the best known contemporary propositions about gender concern differences in the way men and women are said to deal with power. The usual argument is that men are more likely than women to define relationships in terms of power, of who dominates whom – who wins, who loses. For men, it is said, being recognized as having power is more significant than using it. Women, it is said, are inclined to use power but not to claim it. Observed differences in "assertiveness" are said to stem from the greater need of men to be publicly acknowledged as powerful, rather than from any advantage explicit assertiveness provides in influencing the course of events.

To what extent are such propositions reflected in your own experience? In the characters in *Othello*, *Saint Joan*, and *War and Peace*? What are the possible implications for leadership?

5.2

It seems reasonable to assume that a large fraction of the executive talent in the world is found among women. Yet, only a small fraction of high executives in modern firms are women.

1. In what senses is this disparity a problem for a corporation? If you were on a corporate Board of Directors, would you view this situation as a prime concern for the corporation?
2. How did such a disparity happen? If you were a consultant to the Board, what diagnosis would you make of the factors involved?
3. What can be done? If you were the CEO of a corporation and committed to having women as 50 percent of the high executives in the corporation, what steps would you take? What problems would you anticipate?

Would the facts, your analysis, your recommendations, or your feelings be any different if we looked at the fraction of corporate executives who are (a) black – relative to the fraction of people in the world who are black, (b) without college degrees – relative to the fraction of people in the world who are without college degrees, (c) Muslim – relative to the fraction of people in the world who are Muslim, or (d) are short – relative to the fraction of people in the world who are short? Explain.

Would the facts, your analysis, your recommendations, or your feelings be any different if we looked at the female fraction of executives in: (a) military organizations; (b) voluntary organizations;

(c) schools; (d) universities; (e) hospitals; or (f) religious organizations? Explain.

5.3

In modern discussions of men and women as leaders it is often argued that gender, *per se*, is unimportant. That is, being a man or a woman is seen as associated with a host of variables (such as economic or social position, expectations, life experiences) that affect managerial behavior or success, but it is not conceived to be a primary, direct factor. Manifest gender differences are seen as produced by more fundamental factors that are correlated with gender. For example, women and men are portrayed as having different careers in organizations because women and men differ in their economic power, and economic power affects behavior and its interpretation. According to this view, an individual woman who happened to have (or acquire) some specific attribute commonly associated with men as a group (e.g., relative economic independence) would have a career that looked more like the average man than the average woman. A somewhat more complicated version of the argument recognizes that cultural practices reflect past experiences as well as current conditions, thus that a history of significant differences in underlying factors may be encoded into cultural beliefs about gender that are resistant to current changes.

There are alternative views that see gender, *per se*, as much more fundamental. These views take two major forms: In the first form, it is argued that there are inherent gender differences traceable to biology and that these differences are, in fact, more important than such things as economic position, etc. in explaining male–female differences in leadership. A common variant of this perspective is one that emphasizes the implications of hormonal differences for leadership. In the second form, it is argued that sexual differentiation is a fundamental feature of human existence (or the ideological interpretation of that experience) around which human organization is built. A common variant of this perspective is the one that emphasizes sexual identity as the basis for gender competition and the permanent resistance of hegemonic male groups to female equality.

Although it is possible that research or indoctrination will some day resolve the differences in these (and other related) conceptions of the role of gender in leadership, that day seems relatively distant. In the meantime, organizations face day-to-day issues in how to deal with gender in leadership. Are there any possible guidelines for introducing improvements in organizations that are relatively insensitive to what beliefs one has about these underlying "truths"?

5.4

In an interview, Erica Jong said that Henry Miller is better known and more highly regarded in Europe and Japan than he is in the US because American society is puritanical about sex. She argued that Miller understood that spirituality and sexuality were connected, that the body and soul were not discrete (actually the interviewer spelled it "discreet," which may also be true but perhaps is a different point). "To be sexy is to really have a life force," she said. Thus, Erica Jong felt that Henry Miller's attitude toward life gave him (and others who lived and worked around him) tremendous exuberant energies.

Are there ways to enhance, use, or constrain the exuberance and pleasures of sexuality in a modern organization without creating insuperable problems both for the organization and for the social system within which it operates? In particular, what are the possible roles of ambiguity, flirtation, organizational incest taboos, sublimation of sexual drives, and fantasy? Are there gender, age, national, or cultural differences in acceptable enhancements or prohibitions and what are their implications?

5.5

On the basis of her study of a sample of 1,257 working men and women in Los Angeles County, Barbara A. Gutek asserts (in *Sex and the Workplace*) that women use sex at work much less frequently than men do. By that, she means that men talk about sex more and use it for a variety of expressions, particularly exhibiting friendship as well as power toward women and proclaiming their heterosexuality to other men.

How would you account for the differences? Should we be concerned about them? Why or why not? If you wanted to eliminate the differences, would you increase sexual expressiveness at work by women, decrease it by men, or eliminate it altogether? Why? What are the implications for leadership? For life?

5.6

Currently, sexual harassment in the workplace seems to be a larger issue in the US than in most other countries. There are numerous interpretations of these differences, including:

1. Sexual harassment of women by men is a direct consequence of differences between men and women in power. The problems exist everywhere that power differences exist. The reason they are more conspicuous in the US is that American women have achieved a level of political and social power that enables them to expose the harassment without disastrous consequences to themselves. The problem is greater in other countries, but power differences keep it unexposed.

2. American problems of sexual harassment are problems of adolescent attitudes toward sex and sexuality in the US. The American sexual culture is a repressive one in which sexual feelings are viewed as "dirty," shameful, and male. Sex is defined as physically, emotionally, and morally dangerous for a woman, obligatory for a male. As a result, more than in other countries, men are driven to sexual aggressiveness and women are driven to expecting and fearing that aggressiveness.

3. Sexual harassment is a problem of cultural misunderstanding. All relations between the sexes raise sexual possibilities, and those possibilities are explored by verbal and non-verbal exchanges between the sexes. When men and women speak different languages, sexual exchanges are filled with miscommunications and misunderstandings. The misunderstandings are greater in

the US than other countries because of the greater cultural variety in the American work place.

4. The differences between the US and other countries in the problem of sexual harassment is more a difference between "fashion leaders" and "fashion followers" than anything else. The spread of social problems and their recognition (for example, problems of drugs, crime, and sex) around the world is like the spread of fads. The US is often a leader in the creation and identification of such social problems. In time, other countries will imitate.

What other interpretations occur to you? Is there any way of deciding which, if any, of these interpretations contain elements of truth? Does it matter?

CHAPTER 6

IMAGINATION, COMMITMENT, AND JOY: *DON QUIXOTE*[1]

Don Quixote de la Mancha

Don Quixote is, in many ways a strange novel for modern Northern European and North American readers. The context of this book is far removed from our own. Cervantes (b. 1547, d. 1616, on the same day as Shakespeare) was an adventurer who fought as a soldier in the Battle of Lepanto (where Venice and the Christian powers repelled the Turks and destroyed their fleet), which leads us back to the context of *Othello*. Cervantes was a slave in North Africa and made numerous attempts to escape or be exchanged for a ransom. We know that he was a tax collector, was never very rich, and was not admitted into high society (perhaps because of his status as a *converso*, a converted Jew), but that he quickly became a best-selling author.

He drew on a tradition that was, even in his own time, obscure and outmoded: romances about chivalry. He claims to be reconstructing a story from conflicting sources and eye witness accounts; which he "edits" thus sparing us from countless digressions[2] or passages of doubtful importance or veracity. The two volumes of *Don Quixote* were published with a gap of 11 years, after the popularity of the first one had triggered the appearance

---

[1] See the film written by James G. March and directed by Steven Schecter: *Passion and Discipline: Don Quixote's Lessons for Leadership*, Films for the Humanities and Sciences (www.films.com).
[2] When Don Quixote arrives at Don Diego de la Miranda's home, for example, Cervantes writes: "Here the author describes in detail Don Diego's mansion, making an inventory of the entire contents of a rich country gentleman's house, but the translator of this story prefers to pass over these kind of details, which do not contribute to the main aim of this story, which is the truth and not digressions without any interest."

of a follow-up written by another author. The second volume makes several references to this apocryphal sequel and also provides commentaries on the first one.

The novel offers a series of witticisms and extremely colorful scenes, characterized by the chivalrous hallucinations of Don Quixote in which other characters who are encountered along the way take part, either in jest or to save their skin. These episodes of bravura are punctuated by fairly lengthy digressions, (including the stories of the shepherdess Marcella and the princess Micomicona) and philosophical discussions (including Don Quixote's monologues on the Golden Age and on arms and letters, and his dialogue on literature with the scholar Sanson Carrasco).

The character of Don Quixote, drawn with fairly vague biographical precision ("In a place in La Mancha whose name I prefer not to remember . . . a gentleman nearing fifty years of age . . .") and ridiculed (the rusty armor, the cardboard helmet, Rossinante), is, like Natasha in *War and Peace*, totally self-obsessed: his knightly honor and courtly love may appear to be projected toward other people, but in fact they merely serve to confirm the merits of the gallant knight. We know very little about Quixote's companion, Sancho Panza ("a good man (if that title can be given to one who is poor), but with very little grey matter in his skull"): he rides a donkey because he does not like walking and aspires to be a governor but doubts whether a crown would look right on his wife's head. The other characters only appear sporadically.

This "strange" novel is, however, one of the great pieces of literature in the history of Western civilization. In the present context, it gives us the opportunity to ask three important questions about leadership (and life):

1. What is the role of imagination?
2. What motivates and justifies great commitment and action?
3. What is the place of joy and the pleasures of the process?

Imagination

Martin Luther King said: "I say to you today, my friends, that even though we face the difficulties of today and tomorrow, I still have a dream."[3] Dreams, visions, and other fantasies of the imagination are, whatever their level of

---

[3]   Martin Luther King, Jr, "I have a dream," Washington, DC, August 28, 1963.

sophistication, realism, and coherence, a means of freeing ourselves from the restrictions imposed by everyday reality, physical constraints, our limited capacities, and the political and economic context.

They are an ambiguous medium for expressing our aspirations and fears and have a complex relationship with reality. They can be seen as a way of escaping from reality, an opiate for the people that allows them to flee a hostile world made unbearable by their fates or by the malicious sorcerers who bedevil Don Quixote and enter the universe of their desires, just like the little matchstick seller in Hans Christian Andersen's story. Fantasies and visions have great evocative and stimulative power.

In dreams, everybody can be rich, or young if they regret being old, or adult if they hate being a child, or be irresistibly seductive, and everybody can have a string of conquests and end up living in a just world. Dreams make it possible to discover new possibilities or paths toward new realities, playing on the ambiguity of the present (am I not better than I think I am?) and the future (cannot this world become better?). Dreams may not be as realistic as the targets we formulate while we are awake but they have the same effect of pushing us toward audacious actions and motivating us to do things we would not otherwise do.

Dreams and the imagination can also reveal the real essence of things, as in the case of Andrei at Austerlitz or in front of the oak tree. Dreams offer us a vision of a possible new identity or a world that can guide our actions as an instrument of change.[4]

Ignoring the evidence of reality, leaders look for the actualization of an ambitious and far-reaching dream (Joan of Arc, Martin Luther King Jr., Anouar El Sadate, Bronislaw Geremek or Vaclav Havel). They shield that dream from the criticisms of their entourage and from setbacks that seem to prove them wrong, as most interesting visions initially seem to be unrealistic and do not immediately produce results. Leaders often keep their visions intact by reinterpreting the failures that occur when they are first brought to fruition. Revolutionaries and reformers argue that lack of success is the result of not going far enough when putting ideas into practice. Don Quixote invokes the action of malicious sorcerers to explain his failures and thus to protect his actions from reconsideration. Such a course

---

[4] Claude Riveline maintains that the two life-changing phenomena are dreams and mourning. Unlike dreams, however, mourning tends to lead to an adjustment of personal aspirations to the reality of the world. While mourning is therefore a necessary phase in individual growth, dreams are more powerful when it comes to transforming the world.

is obviously dangerous, for it restricts learning from experience; but vision-aries protect themselves from reality by ignoring or reinterpreting it.

A vision is often embodied in one person and sticking to that vision means, by implication, choosing to trust its standard bearer: Steve Jobs at Apple, Bill Gates at Microsoft, etc. How can we ensure that the vision lives on after the visionary has gone? We must be able to dissociate the vision from the person and consider that a visionary sees something before other people do, but is *possessed by* his or her vision (as in the case of Joan of Arc) more than he or she *possesses* it. The vision is then passed on to other converts (something that Don Quixote succeeds in doing when Sancho Panza refuses to accept Quixote's recantation).

How can we encourage the appearance of visions capable of transform-ing the course of history? Unless we want such visions to remain the domain of a few improbable madmen, saints, and geniuses asocial enough to resist the injunctions of a reasonable world, we must be more tolerant about allowing dreams to flourish inside our organizations (and not just those of their leaders). This implies a prevailing culture that looks kindly on dreams and visions and avoids repressing them by invoking accepted truths or experience.

It is unfortunate that studies of visionary leadership focus too much on the lone leader and not enough on the way that he or she can maintain a climate propitious to the blossoming of original visions. Vision will generally only be a motor of change if it can be shared by at least a few people: Saint Joan needed the constable and Dunois to agree to give her adequate responsibilities and Christopher Columbus had to find an Isabel of Castille to pay for his ships. Innovators always need to make some sponsors or investors share their dream.

Visions are something akin to poetic activity. The poet draws on real-ity and imagination, using language to evoke new meanings. Visionary, or poetic, leadership recognizes that life mixes different levels of reality, and leaders act without fully understanding the reasons for it, discovering the meaning of an action through the action itself.

Don Quixote is a visionary. He creates a world in which he rights wrongs and, like Saint Joan, draws other people into the fantasy that he has fash-ioned. That fantasy does not aspire to an ideal social order, but rather to a proper life of beauty and harmony. The need for an arbitrary creation of beauty is exemplified by Quixote's love of Dulcinea, whose attributes are manufactured by his imagination. He invites others to picture her as he pictures her, not because his portrayal is objectively accurate but because he (and they) choose to believe her so.[5] When the traders from Toledo state that they would willingly extol the merits of Dulcinea if Don Quixote were to show her to them, he replies: "what's the virtue in confessing to the truth of something as manifest as a beauty that you can see . . . The essential thing is that without seeing her, you must believe, confess, affirm, swear, and defend it [the truth that Dulcinea is without equal]." (I, 4).

Similarly, he tells the duchess who doubts the existence of Dulcinea: "I behold her as she must necessarily be . . ." (II, 32) The duchess goes on to reply: "henceforth I will believe, and I will see to it that everyone in my house believes, that there is a Dulcinea in El Toboso, and that she is living today, and that she is beautiful and nobly born . . ." (II, 32).

Don Quixote defies ordinary conceptions of reality. He asks whether it is better to accept reality or to invent it, why should we not believe in Dulcinea and in a more beautiful world.[6] Don Quixote's "madness" therefore consists of living in a world that he has created rather than in the one others experience and of not caring about the consequences of his action.

The logic of reality entails two aspects of relevance to a leader. On one hand, reality is complex and our knowledge of it is limited, so we are not sure whether a particular action will achieve our desired goal. This awareness can lead to paralysis (what is the point of doing anything if the results depend on chance?) or cynicism (what is the point of fighting for a better world if we are not certain of the effect of our actions?). On the other hand, reality can be created by action. It need not necessarily be taken as given. This extends to the discourse of a leader: Dulcinea is created by Don Quixote's imagination. Reality is in part a social construction, and interpretation plays an important role in this construction.

Commitment

Myths of heroes occupy a conspicuous place in human beliefs. Confidence in the providential action of great heroes fulfils the human desire for human control of destiny. We attribute to our leaders an essential role in the pageant

[5] Note that this rhetoric is similar to that used 21 years later by Descartes (possibly borrowed from Saint Anselm) in the *Discourse on Method* to prove the existence of God.

[6] Is Don Quixote's approach so different from that of the creators of "back-worlds" criticized by Nietzsche, or from the Promethean dream to build a better and more acceptable world?

of history. We imagine that leaders can make our terrifying world into an enchanted place once more.

According to Fitzroy R. S. Raglan,[7] the typical mythological hero is of royal stock and his birth is, to some degree, miraculous (his mother is sometimes a virgin, or perhaps he is fathered by a god). His father (real or adoptive) is a king and often a close relative of the mother. There is an attempt to kill him at birth (often by his father or maternal grandfather), but he escapes this threat and is taken in and brought up by strangers in a distant country. We know little about his childhood, but when he reaches maturity he returns to his future kingdom. There he defeats the king, or a giant, a dragon, or some other foul beast, marries a princess – often his predecessor's daughter – and becomes king. He reigns in peace and introduces just laws, but one day he loses the favor of the gods or of his subjects, is chased out of the kingdom, and dies mysteriously, often on the top of a hill or mountain (subject to availability). His children do not succeed him. He is not buried, but he has one or several holy shrines.

This saga unfurls throughout the ages in different cultures, with a few local variations. The hero is often depicted as being tough, solitary, and stoical, a warrior and amoral killer aspiring to excellence and a destiny that sets him apart, and he is often possessed by a vision. In short, he is a somewhat asocial, or even antisocial, character.

Our need for heroes (whether positive or negative) makes us bestow this role on great predators of the financial world like Michael Milken, or on creators of business empires like Henry Ford, Alfred Sloan, Steve Jobs, Scott McNealy, and Bill Gates. We applaud their exploits . . . and their eventual downfall. These heroes and geniuses reassure us about the human capacity to affect the course of history. Plutarch, Carlyle, and other hagiographers of great men reassure us by providing us with arguments to counter Tolstoy's vision of the insignificance of human actions.

Heroic leadership demands great action and great commitment. Such commitment is usually justified by expectations of great consequences. This logic of consequences underlies virtually all discussions of motivation, incentives, and decision making in leadership. The assumption is that the great actions that produce great changes in the world are sustained by a belief in their effectiveness.

---

[7]   Fitzroy R. S. Raglan, *The Hero: A Study in Tradition, Myth, and Drama.* Westport, CT: Greenwood Press.

There seems little question that great actions often arise from a feeling that one is capable of getting things moving. This is true of creativity and even of revolutions, which are born less often of "impotent" despair than of the growing power of people bearing seeds of change (the bourgeoisie against the aristocracy, students against the administrative hierarchy, etc.). People who feel that they are effective and recognized as such involve themselves more fully in their organization, participate more in political life, and take more initiatives.

A leader who has already tasted success is willing to take more risks and make more daring decisions. The fact that he or she is expected to succeed gives him or her more slack in carrying out risky experiments and encouraging people to accept a favorable interpretation of the results. The tokens of recognition that organizations give their bosses and the personal credit bestowed on the latter for apparently favorable results, even if these lack real justification, ultimately serve further to stimulate audacious leadership. Although finding oneself successful in the sense of achieving one's aspirations tends to inhibit conscious risk taking, it leads to underestimating the risks one is taking and thus to taking greater risks than are recognized. A culture of success stimulates a culture of exaggerated beliefs in capabilities, and thus an inclination toward risk taking.

Within a consequential logic, where action is motivated by hope of favorable consequences, faith in these potential consequences has to be effectively maintained ("you CAN make a difference") even if this means ignoring the lessons of experience and intelligence. This is achieved via indoctrination (the training of bosses) based on heroic tales of management, the promotion of those who achieve results (even if their personal responsibility for these results is uncertain), an interpretation of history that exaggerates human control, and a sufficient turnover of staff to prevent wise old sages from polluting the faith of newcomers. It is also possible, however, to undertake great actions outside a logic of consequences. An individual can be motivated by his or her faith in God (like Saint Joan) or in the forces of history (like Kutuzov), or by irrational causes (love for Desdemona, revenge for Othello, narcissistic joy for Natasha).

Quixote provides another basis for action – his sense of himself and his identity and the obligations associated with it – a logic of appropriateness. Don Quixote creates a world in which he can live the life he considers appropriate. He draws sustenance from its correspondence with his ideals, without worrying about its consequences. He substitutes a logic of identity for a logic of reality: "I am a knight, and I shall die a knight, if it so pleases the Most High" (II, 32).

Sancho points out that the knights in chivalrous romances had compelling reasons for their actions: "It seems to me that the knights who behaved in this way had provocation and cause for their crazy actions and penances. But what cause has your worship for going mad? What lady has rejected you or what evidence have you found to prove that the lady Dulcinea del Toboso has been trifling with Moor or Christian?"

Don Quixote replies: "For a knight errant to go crazy for a reason merits neither credit nor thanks; the point is to act foolishly without any justification . . . (I, 25)." "Without any justification," he says, meaning without any consequential justification. For he certainly has a justification for his actions. Don Quixote aims to lead a proper life – one that realizes the concept that he has of himself. He follows a logic of identity. This logic consists in acting according to one's own concept of oneself. Action is no longer justified by its consequences, by what one can expect from it. We find ourselves back with Kierkegaard's assertion that a religion that can be justified (in terms of its outcomes) is no longer a religion, or with our earlier discussion about trust, love, and friendship: if they have a rational justification, then they are nothing more than economics. Human beings demonstrate their humanity not by using reason to achieve their goals, but by using their wills in defiance of reason.[8]

Quixote considers himself to be a righter of wrongs, convinced of his unerring duty to discern where justice lies and act appropriately. He justifies his intervention in favor of the galley slaves, for example, by deeming it unjust that they should be punished against their wills (justice rests on the guilty party's approval of his or her sentence). He believes they have been declared guilty either through lack of money and friends or because of corrupt judges, and considers that, if there is one single innocent among them, then this is sufficient reason for all to go unpunished. If some of them then evade their due punishment, it would be unjust for others to be subjected to it. Moreover, justice must ultimately be enforced by those who have suffered and not meted out by brutal guards who have nothing personal against the galley slaves.

---

[8]   Scandals like those of Enron and Worldcom have shown what happens when accountants put the development of their business opportunities (immediate efficiency, utilitarian and opportunistic logic) ahead of the standard practices of their profession (conforming to a social role, the logic of identity).

There should be no mistake. The consequences of Don Quixote's actions are rarely favorable, either to him or to those he attempts to help. He often aggravates the situation of others and emerges in a bad light. Like Pierre Bezukhov with his serfs, his muddle-headed benevolence frequently sows the seeds of disaster. For Quixote, intention is primary in judging virtue; consequences are secondary. It is an emphasis not unknown to other discussions about ethics.[9]

Quixote's sense of himself is echoed by Henry Miller:

> I will begin by saying that the way I spend most of my time is not at all the way I would like to spend it. It's because I am still a man with a conscience – which I am sorry about. I am a man who has regard for his obligations and duties, and these are things I have been fighting against most of my life. I want to say, "Fuck it all, fuck you all, get out of my life." That's how I feel . . . What I mean is that I want to be the opposite of what I am, and yet, to be very frank and honest with you, I am very happy the way I am. I wouldn't want to change. There it is – a frightful contradiction. I admit it shamelessly . . . All of us who have some awareness and some intelligence know that we have to play a role in life . . . You are fulfilled if you play your role to the best of your ability . . . a man who enters into the life we have today and who does it consciously and deliberately enjoys what he's doing . . . When you fully accept something, you are no longer victimized by it. But those are rare men . . .[10]

Don Quixote teaches us that the meaning of life is neither given to us in advance nor discovered, but affirmed by an act of will. He extols commitment, preferring to act ill advisedly when it would be better to abstain than to go to the opposite extreme. When he foolishly, but bravely, confronts the lions, he explains:

> it was my bounden duty to attack the lions I attacked just now, though I knew it to be the height of rashness. I know well the nature of valor, that it is a virtue situated between two vicious extremes, cowardice and

[9]
> If we are tricked and deceived,
> Given bad for good
> By he who knows nothing
> And takes bad for good,
> Is it not for the good that he dies?
> (Louis Aragon, *I protest*)

[10] Henry Miller, *My Life and Times.* Playboy Press, 1971.

temerity. But it will be a lesser evil for a valiant man to rise till he reaches the point of rashness, rather than sink to the point of cowardice. (II, 17)

Although Don Quixote commits himself to an arbitrary personal project, in no way does he defend an individual's right to seek and define his own path. He does not speak for a "self" that is constructed by an egocentric individual but for an individual trying to discern and execute a "self" that is defined by a social/historical process. He sticks to a vision – that of a knight errant – that he does not seek to justify, criticize, or perfect.[11] He teaches us that an action justified by the hope of favorable consequences lacks grace. He loves his lady because it is the lot of a knight errant to pine for a lady. He sees little merit in declaring the perfection of a real lady who truly is perfect.

His world is organized around his involvement in the identity that he has decided to enact:

[Sancho:] but see then, my lord, that I am neither Rodrigo de Narvaez, nor the Marquis of Mantua, but rather Pedro Alonzo, your neighbor; and neither is Your Grace Beaudoin, nor Aben-Darraez, but rather the honest mister Quijada.

I know who I am, replies Don Quixote, yo sé quien soy (I, 5). In those four words, he expresses his central conception of what justifies commitment.

Joy

The Norse sagas tell the story of Olav Trygvason, a great Norwegian warrior of the tenth century. He lived barely 30 years before he was killed in battle, but he fought throughout northern Europe, Ireland, England, Scotland, and Scandinavia. Along the way, he contributed substantially to the conversion of Norway to Christianity; but it is hard to read the sagas without being impressed that Olav Trygvason was driven less by religious zeal or political causes than by the simple joys of fighting. "King Olav was

[11]   Similarly, Antigone does not resist Creon's laws in the name of an inalienable freedom or an individual conscience rising up against unjust oppression, but rather acts in the name of sacred values decreeing her obligations to the dead in her family. As Anouilh shows, without betraying Sophocles, she is a conservative who sets the arbitrariness of religion against the more modern arbitrariness of reasons of state.

the gladdest of all men and very playful, blithe and forgiving . . . his foes
he tormented much; some he burned, some he let wild hounds tear
asunder, and others he maimed or cast down from high mountains . . .
Heaven and earth will burst before a leader such as the joyful Olav is
born."

Leadership offers several types of pleasures:

- The pleasure of becoming a leader, as regards both promotion and success in competition for the post.
- The pleasures connected with the role (chairing meetings, being the
  source of approval, giving orders, taking decisions, receiving delegations,
  granting favors, managing crises), with being in the thick of the action
  (knowing what is going on better than other people, seeing the under-
  side of cards, experiencing the theatrical buzz of meetings or negotia-
  tions), with an exciting life, and with the self-confidence derived from
  the value that people attach to the time and attention of a leader.
- The pleasure of being recognized as a leader, connected with the
  confirmation of a prestigious status, with a flashy business card, with
  fame, deference (one becomes wise, sensible, clever, sexy), and treats
  (money, perks, first-class plane tickets).

It is often, therefore, easier to understand certain aspects of leaders' behavior by focusing on the pleasures that they can gain from their actions rather
than on the consequences they achieve.

We are ambivalent about the importance of the pleasures of action,
criticizing not only those who forget their long run goals and live "without a care for tomorrow," but also those who only think in the long term
and sacrifice all the pleasures of existence for a pot of gold at the end of
the rainbow. In American culture there is a confrontation between a glorification of consumption (as opposed to the pleasures of creation and con-
templation) and a Puritan tradition that sees pleasure as sinful and only
tolerates play or games as serious, planned, organized, and optimized activities. So, leadership is portrayed sometimes as a pleasant activity, sometimes
as evangelism, sometimes as a pursuit of personal recognition, sometimes
as a solemn acceptance of overwhelming responsibilities, sometimes as
a chance to strengthen self-esteem, sometimes as only fit for self-obsessed
workaholics.

Don Quixote simultaneously celebrates a commitment to a sense of self
and to the realization of joy. The book is a comic masterpiece. Whereas

tragedy confirms that life has a meaning and that Man's victory over adversity is imaginable, but thwarted by powerful forces, comedy prefers to scoff at human follies and eccentricities.

This derision is a response to the absurdity of the human condition but it does not presuppose any hostility. Although we laugh at Don Quixote's misadventures and his pretensions, this does not prevent us from liking him and being grateful for him, just as several of the characters in the book do and are.

When the bachelor Sansón Carrasco (the Knight of the White Moon) tells Don Antonio Moreno how after first failing to defeat Quixote in combat, he finally did in order to get him to agree to return home to be cured, Don Antonio says: "O, señor, may God forgive you the wrong you have done the whole world in trying to bring the most amusing madman in it back to his senses. Do you not see, señor, that what is gained by restoring Don Quixote's sanity can never equal the enjoyment his delusions give?" (II, 65).

We laugh at Don Quixote because he is funny, but we do not scorn him. He reminds us of our own insignificance and our own ridiculousness. Nowadays, we tend to disapprove of laughter directed at madmen. Mockery is approved only when aimed at powerful people. We admire Don Quixote, however, even as we laugh at him, for he represents an ideal of joy. He turns his life into a work of art by choosing a role and taking it to its limits.

Throwing oneself into a role gives three types of esthetic pleasure: First, the direct experience of the joys inherent to our situation – the intoxication of power, the exaltation of being in love, the sensual pleasure of feeling alive. Second, the irony derived from enjoying the derisory aspect of this role, the fundamental ridiculousness of all our own pretensions. And, third, the affirmation, appreciation, and acceptance of our role. While being conscious of the limits and absurdities of our position, we discover its beauty and take on our responsibilities, our loves, and our life.

Cervantes glorifies laughter, not because comedy must serve a serious aim, such as teaching us something, but because laughter is fundamental. It allows us to go beyond our tragic condition, to understand the human condition better by recognizing that life is intrinsically funny. Cervantes shows us that Don Quixote's friends are not really doing anything wrong by making fun of him, but in fact are contributing to a joyful life; he is telling us that life is a laughing matter and that the clown is a hero.

Henry Miller wrote:

> Joy is like a river, it flows ceaselessly. It seems to us that this is the message which the clown is trying to convey to us, that we should participate through ceaseless flow and movement, that we should not stop to reflect, compare, analyze, possess, but flow on and through, endlessly like magic. This is the gift of surrender, and the clown makes it symbolically. It is for us to make it real. . . . At no time in the history of man has the world been so full of pain and anguish. Here and there, however, we meet with individuals who are untouched, unsullied, by the common grief. They are not heartless individuals, far from it! They are emancipated beings. For them the world is not what it seems to us. They see with other eyes. We say of them that they have died to the world. They live in the moment, fully, and the radiance which emanates from them is the perpetual song of joy.[12]

Lessons from Quixote

Don Quixote celebrates imagination, commitment, and joy. He reminds us of how ambiguous reality is and how it can be subject to numerous interpretations. He thus makes us aware of certain absurdities in the life of a leader, and of the sympathy that we must therefore have for this role and for the people who play it; but he also shows us the comic nature of the posturing and pretension of leaders . . . and others. Leadership can be considered as an arbitrary, joyful, and unjustifiable commitment. The pleasure of its gratuitousness must be appreciated, and leaders must be distinguished by the elegance and enthusiasm with which they play their role. In this case, they have the chance not only to contribute to the beauty of the world by creating a reality that values individuals and the human race as a whole, but also to discover themselves through action.

Don Quixote's limitations originate from his loss of contact with reality. He is only concerned about himself and pays no attention to the real needs of other people. His inclination to pay attention only to the intentions of an action and to neglect its consequences is potentially disasterous. His constant desire to impose his will on reality emancipates him from any social or practical control, making him a danger to his environment. He depends on the benevolence of other people and, despite his apparent

---

[12] Henry Miller, *The Smile at the Foot of the Ladder.* Duell, Sloan, and Pearce, 1948.

lack of egoism, he lives, like Natasha, as a parasite. He would not, therefore, know how to make himself an example to be followed. The world also
needs common sense. However, we should not infer from this that Don
Quixote should not exist. On the contrary, we must make sure that we protect the Don Quixotes of this world, who make our lives more worth living.

From this point of view, someone who is asked why he or she aspires
to a position of power should let it be known that it is because of a belief
in the values of chivalrous honor, in the pleasures associated with the role
of leader, and in the purity and beauty of Lady Dulcinea of Toboso. And
most of all he or she should try every day to be able to say, with Quixote:
I know who I am.

Queries

6.1

IMAGINATIONS

Imaginations steal the covers from timidity,
Releasing ancient kinds of smells to lure us
Into tasting some warm flavors
From the oysters of our minds.

But what is gained from culinary play
When our elaborate dinner's done
And we return to plainer places
Where we stay at night?

Why should we set those hungers free,
Assaulting cautious dreams
That you and I have kept
Cocooned in probity?

We are not old enough
To pass temptations by,
Nor young enough
To travel with them far.
(J. G. March, *Minor Memos* (1990))

What is the role of caution in illusions, dreams, and fantasy? Why is the poem's structure concealed? What is the relevance for leadership? For life?

6.2

ON BEING A PATSY

Most of my enemies,
And all of my friends.
Are clever enough
To fool me seven ways
Before breakfast.

Often they do,
Though not always
With intention.
They lie; they flatter;
They cheat.
They have funny memories
Of little things
We made together.
I suppose I do, too.

Expectations of virtue
Are a fool's fantasy.
I trust you,
Not because you can be trusted,
But because you should be.
(J. G. March, *Academic
Notes* (1974))

What are the implications of such a perspective for leadership? What are the prospects? What are the problems?

6.3

The modern vision of *Don Quixote* is found not in written fiction but in film, and the contemporary Cervantes is Woody Allen. His loving enthusiasm for, and unremitting laughter at, the myths of modern manhood and modern urban life are classic celebrations of both our pretensions and their absurdities. By encouraging us to recognize the ridiculousness of contemporary codes of honor and yet to embrace those codes with affection and commitment, he provides an elegant metaphor for life as a modern leader.

Comment on three things:

1. Whether this is a reasonable characterization of Woody Allen's films.
2. Whether, if it is, there is any significant similarity between Quixote and Allen.
3. Whether the messages of the films are relevant for modern leaders.

6.4

Cervantes frequently interrupts his narrative of the adventures of Don Quixote to provide stories that appear to have rather little to do with the rest of the book. One such story is that of Marcela and Grisóstomo (I, 12–14). The story describes the beautiful shepherdess, Marcela: "When she reached the age of fourteen or fifteen, whoever beheld her blessed God for having made her so beautiful, and most of them were hopelessly in love with her."

Among the men who fell hopelessly in love with Marcela was Grisóstomo, who is described as: "unrivaled in wit, unequaled in courtesy, unapproached in gentle bearing, a paragon of friendship, generous without limit, grave without arrogance, merry without vulgarity, and, in short, first in all that constitutes goodness . . ."

Marcela rejects Grisóstomo, and he dies of a broken heart. Grisóstomo's friends (and Grisóstomo in his poem) indict Marcela for complicity in his death, claiming that she had to accept responsibility for the effects of her beauty. She appears and pleads her case. Quixote supports Marcela.

What is the basis for the indictment? What are Marcela's arguments in response? Granting that most of us would probably also side with

Marcela and Quixote in the immediate case, is there any merit at all in the logic of Grisóstomo's argument? What are its general implications for people of beauty or other virtues (e.g., wisdom, youth, wealth, status, power)? For leaders?

6.5

In Chapter 31 of the second part of Don Quixote, we are introduced to "a grave ecclesiastic, one of those who rule noblemen's houses; one of those who, not being born magnates themselves, never know how to teach those who are, how to behave as such; one of those who would have the greatness of the great measured by their own narrowness of mind; one of those who, when they try to introduce economy into the household they rule, lead it into stinginess."

At dinner, the ecclesiastic first attacks the duke for encouraging Don Quixote, then attacks Quixote, telling him to go home and stop all this nonsense. Don Quixote replies (in Chapter 32) in a speech in which he says: "Knight I am, and knight I will die . . ." After a while, the ecclesiastic says he can no longer endure such foolishness and leaves the table.

Don Quixote is considerably aggrieved by the attack, but (taking his cue from the duke) he does not pursue the ecclesiastic to demand satisfaction. He explains to Sancho, the duke, and the duchess why he does not do so. In the course of that explanation, Quixote distinguishes between an "offense" or "wrong" (agravio) and an "insult" or "affront" (afrenta), arguing that the latter would require him to respond physically, but the former did not.

What is the difference between an "agravio" and an "afrenta" in Quixote's formulation? Why is it important to him? What are possible implications for understanding contemporary organizational leadership?

6.6

When Quixote meets the traders from Toledo, he insists that they recognize the unique beauty of Dulcinea. When they protest that they have never seen the lady, he says that there would be no virtue in their admitting to her beauty if they had seen her. You must swear to it "without seeing her," he says.

When Sancho challenges him to provide consequential reasons for his crazy behavior, Quixote says that providing such reasons merits "neither credit nor thanks," that one should act foolishly without justification.

What is Quixote's point? What are its implications for modern life and leadership?

CHAPTER 7

PLUMBING AND POETRY

We started by looking skeptically at leadership. It is not at all clear that leadership requires any remarkable talents, or that major differences in the success of organizations reflect differences in the capabilities of their leaders, or that history is the product of leaders' actions. Leadership – and our relationship to it – are important, however, if society is to function properly and if leaders themselves – and those under them – are to feel at ease.

Improving the practice of leadership is, therefore, a major challenge. It is equally important to reflect on the relationship between individual well being and leadership, so that leaders can come to terms with their ambition for power, the obligations that leadership entails, and the dependence that it engenders. In this way, a commitment to a career as a leader, or to working alongside a leader, becomes both socially useful and personally gratifying.

The argument here has been that the essential problems facing a leader are quite simply the problems of life: How can we make ethical and aesthetic sense of our lives? How can we reconcile a rich personal life and public responsibilities? How can we encourage creativity and imagination without paying the price for the stupid ideas they engender? How can we find a balance between the advantages and disadvantages associated with diversity and unity? How can we create an equilibrium between ambiguity and coherence? What are the costs of an order based on the relationship between power and subordination, and what are the alternatives? How do elements associated with sexuality and gender affect our behavior? How do we keep ourselves motivated? How can we reconcile imagination, dreams, and vision with an awareness of reality? How do the pleasures of life affect the results of our actions, our lifestyles, and the significance that we give to our life?

This list is obviously incomplete, and we have introduced a few major themes in order to discuss them, not to find solutions for them. Each of us builds his or her own view of leadership around these themes.

There are two essential dimensions of leadership: "plumbing," i.e., the capacity to apply known techniques effectively, and "poetry," which draws on a leader's great actions and identity and pushes him or her to explore unexpected avenues, discover interesting meanings, and approach life with enthusiasm.

The plumbing of leadership involves keeping watch over an organization's efficiency in everyday tasks,[1] such as making sure the toilets work and that there is somebody to answer the telephone. This requires competence, not only at the top but also throughout all the parts of the organization; a capacity to master the context (which supposes that the individuals demonstrating their competence are thoroughly familiar with the ins and outs of the organization); a capacity to take initiatives based on delegation and follow-up; a sense of community shared by all the members of the organization, who feel they are "all in the same boat" and trust and help each other; and, finally, an unobtrusive method for coordination, with each person understanding his or her role sufficiently well to be able to integrate into the overall process and make constant adjustments to it.[2]

These aspects are essential for the smooth operation of organizations, but they do not appear in most treatises on leadership, no doubt because they are too mundane or too closely linked to a precise context and specific techniques. In order for the world to be able to benefit from a few Don Quixotes and the rare Joans of Arc, it needs plenty of Sancho Panzas and Dunoises.

Leadership also requires, however, the gifts of a poet, in order to find meaning in action and render life attractive. The formulation and dissemination of interesting interpretations of reality form the basis for constructive collective action. A leader is equipped with the power and words for this purpose. If power is not used as an instrument for winning personal influence, but as a means of encouraging other people to blossom, its charms can be enjoyed while the fear that it inspires is minimized. Words

---

[1] All these points are discussed in detail in "Mundane organizations and heroic leaders," reproduced in Appendix 2.

[2] Project-management studies refer to this as being able to "adjust in time."

allow us to forge visions and poetic language, through its evocative power, allow us to say more than we know, to teach more than we understand.

A leader must know how to appreciate life and be aware of reality, without falling into the cynicism and bitterness that can arise from the knowledge that our efforts are probably in vain. He or she must know how to savor the charms of simple joys and appreciate the glory of human willpower.

Human willpower is that which allows us to commit ourselves unreservedly and unconditionally (like Desdemona, whose love for Othello remains constant even when he is ruining her life), to act without any justification, to love the unlovable, to trust the untrustworthy, and to believe the incredible, to be able to say: "I know who I am."

The course on which this book is based usually concluded with a quotation from Etienne Pivert de Senancour: L'homme est périssable. Il se peut; mais périssons en résistant, et, si le néant nous est reservé, ne faisons pas que ce soit une justice. [Man is perishable. That may be. But let us perish resisting; and if nothingness is what awaits us, let us not act in such a way that it is a just fate.][3]

Query

7.1

A menudo se atribuyen estos pensamientos a Jorge Luis Borges:	These thoughts are often attributed to Jorge Luis Borges:
Si pudiera vivir nuevamente mi vida . . .	If I could live my life again . . .
En la próxima	In the next
trataría de cometer más errores.	I would try to commit more errors.
No intentaría ser tan perfecto,	I would not try to be so perfect,
me relajaría más.	I would relax more.
Sería más tonto de lo que he sido,	I would be more foolish than I have been,
de hecho tomaría muy pocas cosas con seriedad.	in fact I would take very few things seriously.
Sería menos higiénico,	I would be less hygienic,
correría más riesgos,	run more risks,

---

[3] Etienne Pivert de Senancour, *Obermann*, 1804, letter XC.

haría más viajes;	take more trips;
contemplaría más atardeceres,	I would contemplate more late afternoons,
subiría más montañas;	I would climb more mountains;
nadaría más ríos.	I would swim more rivers.
Iría a más lugares	I would go to more places
adonde nunca he ido,	where I have never been,
comería más helados	I would eat more ice cream
y menos habas. . . .	and fewer beans. . . .
Si pudiera volver atrás	If I could go back
trataría de tener	I would try to have
solamente buenos momentos.	only good moments.
Por si lo saben,	For as they say,
de eso está hecha la vida,	that is what life is made of
sólo de momentos. . . .	only moments. . . .
Si pudiera volver a vivir	If I could live again
comenzaría a andar descalzo	I would start to walk barefoot
a principios de la primavera	at the beginning of spring
y seguiría así	and I would continue that way
hasta cocluir el otoño.	until the autumn ends.
Daría más vueltas en calesita,	I would take more rides in an open carriage,
contemplaría más amaneceres	contemplate more daybreaks
y jugaría con más niños,	and play with more children,
si tuviera otra vez la vida por delante.	if I had life ahead of me again

Why are such sentiments reserved for the elderly? What are the possible implications for leadership?

APPENDIX 1

INTELLIGENCE VERSUS REASON: AN OVERVIEW OF JAMES MARCH'S WORK

Thierry Weil

Miseries of Reason

*Limited rationality or the critique of pure reason
(from rational decision making to appropriate routine)*

The Enlightenment freed Man from obscurantist myths and substituted Reason as his guide. Nowadays, we know how to put our (supposedly excellent and unbiased) capacity for reasoning at the service of our desires, which are supposedly readily identifiable, consistent, and socially tolerable. In any case, when we have to decide whether to take one course of action rather than another, *we weigh up the consequences of each possible decision and choose the one that will give us the greatest satisfaction.*

Company presidents are ordinary rational people, whose decisions affect their entire organizations; citizens, are also rational agents when they vote for the program that suits them best, trying to assure that the social contract favors their interests as much as possible or seeking to renegotiate it. However, even in situations where sociological and institutional factors seem to play little part, the behavior observed in individuals, and even more in organizations, is far removed from what we would expect from this classical theory of rational decision making.

One of the primary causes of this "irrational" behavior is the fact that the application of reason implies enormous cognitive capacities, beyond the reach of individuals. Who can possibly make a full reckoning of all the options available? Who can calculate all their consequences (either with certainty in cases where we know everything that stems from a choice, or alternatively in terms of expected values where outcomes are known only up to a probability distribution)? How can we then go on to compare all the imaginable determining factors in the world in the light of our own preferences? And how can we decide between short-term and long-term interests if some choices are immediately beneficial but prove prejudicial later on? Will we have the same preferences in the future? Can we predict how these will evolve?

It is clear that, even if a person sticks to the ideal of rational, consequentialist agency that is the basis of microeconomic theories, he or she will be able to apply, at best, only a *limited rationality*. Far from achieving a complete grasp of all the alternatives available (or open to construction), we are confronted with a series of decision-making opportunities. We have an idea of what constitutes a *satisfactory result* for each one of these. If the first course of events envisaged leads to this satisfactory result, all the better, and we stick with this. If this is not the case, then we look for alternatives, in the hope of finding one that satisfies us. If, despite our efforts, we do not find it, or if factors out of our control mean that the result falls below our standards, it is possible that we will reconsider our targets and redefine what we mean by success.

Usually, we will try to save the time needed to make an exhaustive list of possible choices and instead apply procedures we have used successfully in the past in similar situations. We tend to identify the nature of the problem we are confronting and find a suitable approach in our "tool box" of tried and tested methods. We can also look for an appropriate solution outside our own past experience by considering the practices of our professional community, asking ourselves how a proper lawyer/student/teacher/accountant would act in such a situation. In this way we reject *consequentialist rationality*, based on the calculation of optimal choice, in favor of a *logic of appropriateness*: the application of rules that seem to suit the situation.

Organizations face the same problems, although these are hugely complicated by the fact that decisions are not made by one single individual with access to all the available information and with a single, more or less consistent, set of preferences. Some are made in specific departments, following their own particular logics, which depend on the information at hand, the environment, or the people with whom the department normally has contact: a sales department is more sensitive than others to the needs of customers, a financial department more closely attuned to the needs of bankers and shareholders, a production department to those of workers, and a purchasing department to those of suppliers. A company works more as a *political coalition* than as a hierarchical organization guided by one single will.

An organization, even more than an individual, will resort to (sometimes implicit) *procedures* to decide that a particular problem calls for a particular department, a specific procedure or approach. It reduces the complexity of the decisions that have to be made by neglecting the links among different decisions, which are made sequentially or separately: the production department reduces costs by limiting a product's functionality or quality, on the basis of its experience or indications received from marketing, while the sales department establishes the sale price. This lack of coordination thrives even more when there is a certain room for maneuver that renders generally sub-optimal results tolerable. If this slack is used up, however, some decisions will have to be reconsidered.

Other surprises lurk in the gap between the predictions of a rational choice model choice and the reality of an organization's actions. As Søren Christensen succinctly points out, "The very notion of decision is a theory. It supposes that there is a close connection between activities called decision processes, announcements called decisions, and actions called implementations of decisions."[1]

*The application of appropriate procedures or
the critique of practical reason
(why the process does matter as well as the outcome;
from first level routine selection and application to
evolution and learning processes)*

The application of appropriate procedures in the way we have just described can be seen as a highly specific example of consequentialist rationality. In situations where the methods of rational choice take up time, energy, or

[1]   James G. March and Johan P. Olsen, *Ambiguity and Choice in Organization*, Bergen, Norway: Universitetsforlaget, 1976, chapter 16.

money in order to collect and process information, it is *rational* to resort to a procedure that is more economical while yielding results that are not greatly inferior. *Reciprocally,* resorting to classic decision theory can be seen as the *application of appropriate procedures* when there is no other routine or behavior available to handle successfully this kind of situation. Each decision mode can therefore be described as a specific case of the other mode. The specific *behaviors* involved in using the two methods are nonetheless sufficiently different to allow the distinction to be sustained empirically. Observation shows evidence for both in actual behavior. The application of procedures is clearly important to actual organizational behavior.

Some consider, however that the precise behavior of decision makers (evaluating consequences or following rules) is not a relevant issue, since what really matters is that efficient decisions are made. Economists and other functionalists argue that individuals or organizations that come closest to the (by construction optimal) results achieved via rational decision making gain substantial competitive advantage. This evolutionist argument enables them to declare that *the choice made by those best equipped for survival is the same as the one that would have resulted from a rational decision making process,* even if the actual mechanism of decision is different. This difference does not matter for them, since their theories focus on the *result* and not on the *process* that led them to it. Their argument (that survivors will, in one way or another, have made the same decisions as would have rational decision makers), however, relies on the unproven hypothesis that history is efficient, i.e., that it quickly selects the individuals and organizations that are best adapted to their environment. But there is abundant evidence that this assumption is often wrong. Indeed, our environment is flexible enough to allow individuals and organizations with quite different forms or behaviors to coexist on a long-term basis. Similar levels of performance can be achieved in countless ways. Temporary states of quasi-equilibrium largely depend on past history and specific circumstances.

Also, even if history were efficient enough for this equilibrium to be reached in the long term, *the processes that make us reach it are nevertheless important,* since a greater understanding of these processes allows us to identify opportunities to *guide evolution* and promote favorable *change* – for example, by encouraging, among several possible equilibria, the ones that best respond to certain criteria independent of economic efficiency, such as beauty or justice.

Furthermore, improvement of the performances of the pool of competing players does not result only from the banishment of the least competent ones. Individuals and organizations have the capacity to adapt and improve their behavior if they know how to learn from their successes and failures, or if they know how to imitate the behavior of those who achieve greater success than them. Evolution in ecologies of organizations depends not only on random and often unfavorable mutations, but also on each individual's and organization's capacity to learn from experience, which is related to the process of understanding their environment and making decisions.

Individuals and organizations both respond *in the short term* to the problems posed by their environment *by identifying the procedure that seems appropriate to these problems,* and only in exceptional circumstances by applying the techniques of decision theory. *In the longer term, they adapt by learning,* by trying out and evaluating new procedures or adjusting the ones they already use, particularly when none of the procedures available is satisfactory.

Thwarted learning or the critique of dialectic reason

Experiential learning in organizations is based on a cycle in which individuals observe and interpret the environment, then create a model for the functioning of the world and work out their own personal preferences, then go on to influence the decisions of the organization, and finally develop their knowledge by analyzing the way the actions of an organization impact its wider context.

This mechanism for individual and collective learning is, however, undermined by a number of ambiguities. People's actions are not solely determined by their beliefs about the world, but also depend on the role assigned to them within an organization. The decisions of an organization are only loosely linked both to the desires of the participants in the decision-making process on the one hand and the effective application of those decisions on the other hand. Perceptible changes in its environment are not entirely due to an organization's actions, but are also affected by those of other surrounding organizations, or even by totally independent factors. The interpretation of these ambiguous events is itself a social phenomenon that depends on the observer's relationship with other members of the organization: we see what we expect to see (autoconditioning) and what other people whose opinion we value see (social conditioning).

A great deal of March's work therefore focuses on breakdowns in learning and the ways to remedy them, for the merits of learning must be evaluated not by comparing learning to some ideal rules for action but on the basis of the alternatives available. Learning as the way organizations adapt to their environments is thus like democracy, which was said to be the worse regime with the exception of all other ones.

Another complication for learning in organizations comes from *interaction among the different players* and the entanglement of different forms of learning. Thus, an organization's evaluation of two alternative technologies depends on what has already been learned: an organization can thoroughly master a technology with limited potential, while passing over a more promising option due to lack of expertise.

Similarly, some simple models show that, in certain conditions, an organization in which everybody reacts rationally to the results of collective action by working within the parameters under their control will be less efficient than an organization in which some members do not adapt immediately, or adapt at a point when other people have stabilized their behavior.[2]

Other models[3] demonstrate that an organization that rewards those of its members who best apply its procedures, but is also prepared to act on better results obtained through less strict compliance with these procedures, will sometimes benefit from taking on deviants whose beliefs diverge from those of the organization. In fact, such people, even if they often perform poorly, could at some point display the behavior most suited to a particular situation, especially if the environment changes. An organization's capacity to adapt therefore depends on including individuals who learn its standardized behavior slowly, whether through blundering, stubbornness, or altruism.

The technology of foolishness or the critique of immediate reason

In other words, effective learning sometimes entails going beyond the framework of tried and tested solutions, but a daring decision is almost always ineffective in the short term. On the one hand, once a certain degree of competence has been attained, most new ideas are not as good as existing practices. On the other, even if a particular new procedure is potentially

---

[2] Pertti H. Lounamaa and James G. March, "Adaptive coordination of a learning team," *Management Science*, 33 (1987) 107–23.

[3] James G. March, "Exploration and exploitation in organizational learning," *Organization Science*, 2 (1991) 71–87.

an improvement, the competence already acquired in using established procedures means that the latter are more efficient, in the short run, than superior technology used without experience. It has taken time for the use of a computer to improve the performance of a good secretary, it takes time to recoup the effort of learning to use a more modern machine or administrative software package, and it will take time to reap the benefits of interface tools that are more functional than a qwerty keyboard.

Exploring solutions that are mostly inefficient, at least temporarily and often even steadily, demands a degree of playfulness, as well as a love of adventure and risk, but these qualities are discouraged by a "good education." Persisting with alternatives that *may* – but equally may not – turn out to be profitable, despite the warnings and sanctions of an institution or of society, requires obstinacy, or even foolishness.

Who but a fool (or at least an enthusiast) refuses to listen to reason – whether for the sake of provocation or vocation – and doggedly perseveres in his or her errors? That is obviously what Don Quixote does, when declaring that he acts without any thought of reward: "As it has fallen to my lot to be a member of the knight-errantry, I cannot avoid attempting all that seems to me to come within the sphere of my duties."

This "foolishness" makes it possible, not only to explore hitherto unknown alternatives, but sometimes also to discover one's preferences. March indeed rejects the axiom stipulating that individuals have coherent and predefined preferences, so that any inconsistence in their choices would be attributed to a lack of reflection or introspection. This is the paradigm that psychotherapists refer to when they urge their patients to "find themselves." March proposes that individuals *construct their preferences through action*, with their unique personal trials leading them to explore behavior in which they will find a degree of pleasure (if only from the recognition they earn). This is what parents secretly have in mind when they encourage their children to "discover" the joys of reading, helpfulness, and politeness, thus shamelessly frustrating their spontaneous attitudes.

Splendors of Reason

The charms of orthodoxy

Reason is just one of several tools of intelligence (and an overrated one), but March nevertheless knows how to appreciate its qualities. Before criticizing and dismissing the dominant paradigm, he displays all its strengths. He uses a very rational, scientific framework to demonstrate the limits of reason and the need to complement this fine tool with other approaches, such as foolishness or an "immediately" irrational insistence on exploring dangerous paths.

There is no mysticism in March's books on decision-making, nor is there anything whimsical in his thorough description of the procedural rationality of the head of sales in a department store to illustrate the behavioral theory of the firm. March uses the tools of reason to demonstrate the incompleteness of reason, just as Gödel used the axioms of formal logic to formulate the proofs of its incompleteness.

The rigorous and efficient use of reason

Speculating about the future is pointless without using correct reasoning. Thus, March subjected all his social sciences students in Irvine to a relatively advanced mathematics course (with a special emphasis on the handling of statistics) and taught them the art of elaborating rigorous models, and to avoid falling in love with their own hypotheses.

March's scientific discussions are closely argued. Whenever possible, at least in its early work, conjectures are validated by different independent approaches. Reservations about the validity of assumptions and conjecture are thoroughly and clearly discussed. There has been a transition from the former attitude to the latter over the course of March's career, however – the established professor, having nothing left to prove, is more willing to indulge in pure speculation, refusing to claim any relevance.

March does not mix up different genres of text; his scientific books are written with utmost rigor and he leaves to his six volumes of poetry the function of signifying more than he can write. It is this respect for genre that probably prevented him from writing a synthesis of his course on leadership, as no classical format seems equipped to convey the atmosphere of his lectures centered on a free commentary on some literary classics (*Othello, Don Quixote*, George Bernard Shaw's *Saint Joan*, and *War and Peace*), not out of affectation, but because great writers have succeeded in depicting human beings grappling with their incoherencies better than any researcher in the social sciences.

Systemic reason or the quest for intelligence

Just as March rationally demonstrates that a classic rational choice cannot fulfill its objectives, it is in the name of reason that he proposes another means of achieving a goal – intelligence in organizations. It is therefore by virtue of a systemic rationality that he proposes to complete the toolbox of limited classical rationality, as well as complementing the usual forms of procedural rationality with a technology of playfulness and foolishness.

Redemption through Enthusiasm

The collective need for individual gambles

We have seen that the inability to fall back on rational choices in overly complex cognitive situations or to find suitable procedures in new environments leads an individual or organization to adapt by exploring new avenues. Generally speaking, however, this exploratory activity is dangerous, with the most profitable strategy often consisting of imitation of existing procedures that were discovered by others and appear to be efficient.

This does, of course, still render it necessary to have, somewhere in the population, explorers to imitate – individuals who are sufficiently adventurous or sufficiently stupid to stray from the beaten path and sufficiently stubborn to keep going long enough to discover whether their new path actually leads anywhere.

How to make the challenge of exploration attractive

If variations are almost always less efficient than tried and tested methods, particularly in the beginning, how can we encourage exploration? We can start by handsomely rewarding the few explorers who achieve success. This can foster explorations in others, particularly if they are dissatisfied with their lot. It is also possible to reward interesting failures (although this situation demands rare virtue from whoever decides about the reward); not because they are failures, *per se*, but because they open the door to solutions that enrich our knowledge. Finally, we can manipulate potential adventurers' expectations of triumph by recounting success stories.

None of these methods works very well, but some people fortunately become explorers all the same, not because they have any illusions about the gratification that it will give them, but because they are motivated by feelings other than the desire for immediate reward.

Beyond rationality: Poetry, intuition, and enthusiasm

Even though the social sciences sometimes ignore it, we often act for reasons other than reason. We are trying to become the people we would like to be, without any expectation of an immediate reward. We embark on a journey for the intrinsic pleasure of traveling rather than for the rewards of its possible destination.

Intelligence does not consist only in exploiting the world to satisfy our wants. What criterion would we use for this, anyway, as our tastes are not predefined and are partly formed by our actions? We also seek a better understanding of this world of ours in order to make more sense, and therefore enhance our enjoyment, of our lives in it. The richness of our intelligence in this regard partly determines the richness of our actions and the beauty of our lives. Our actions, and the satisfaction we get from them, often depend more on our representations of reality than on reality itself and its problematic interpretation.

Institutions are not based on haggling alone. Just as the social sciences seek to explain behavior in the field of individual action by investigating individual interests (utilitarian rationality), so the political sciences tend to explain the formation of institutions as the result of a social contract negotiated in the best interests of all parties concerned. This theory does not guarantee, however, that such institutions will be efficient. How can we ensure that institutions created and governed in this way acknowledge the interests of those who have no political weight – paupers with no resources to contribute to useful coalitions, unorganized people who are not members of any formal group, and, above all, future generations, excluded from the debate because they have not yet been born?

In contrast to this aggregative concept of a haggling match in which everybody struggles for recognition within the structure of institutions, there is also an integrative tradition, in line with the logic of appropriateness and community, in which the faculty of reasoning is used not to haggle for one's own benefit, but rather to determine the principles and values that bind a community together and to establish the rights that the latter will guarantee each of its members.

A usable theory of political action must take into account these two traditions, and the way in which the institutions that supply the framework indispensable to political life emerge, evolve, and adapt.

Irrelevant actions

March has therefore demonstrated the insufficiencies of utilitarian reason on both a descriptive level – it does not take into account most of the behavior we can observe – and a prescriptive one – if reason were the basis of our actions, we would swiftly lose our capacity for adaptation and create unviable institutions. He goes further than that, however, and shows us that, in a complex, disconcerting, and ambiguous world in which our actions impact on those of other people and undergo countless unforeseen developments, we can only very rarely have significant influence on the course of events that affect us, despite what we – and specially leaders among us – might wish to believe.

Optimism without hope

In this absurd universe, there is great temptation to wallow in helplessness and powerlessness or become cynical and irresponsible. Three attitudes do, however, make it possible to find the motivation required for everyday activities. *Pessimism without despair* starts from the premise that, even if our influence is slight, we can practice damage limitation through unobtrusively devoting ourselves to useful, everyday tasks and thereby render our immediate environment less hostile. This perspective is embodied by Ivan Denisovich,[4] as he celebrates another day spent in the gulag without any harassment or catastrophe. In contrast, *indifference without loss of faith* is based on the observation that, despite the insignificance of most of our actions, opportunities (not always predictable ones) do arise and unexpected crossroads can appear, such that even relatively minimal actions can

---

[4] Alexander Solzhenitsyn, *One Day in the Life of Ivan Denisovich.* New York: Signet Classics, 1998.

modify the course of events. This is embodied by Kutuzov observing the Battle of Borodino and, through the trust that he manifests, keeping up the morale of the officers – the only useful, but potentially determinant, course of action he can follow in the general confusion of the battle. The third attitude is one of *optimism without hope* – that of Don Quixote acting as a knight errant for the sake of the beauty of the world and the exhilaration of living what he feels to be his vocation, thereby accomplishing the obligations that he wants to be worthy enough to fulfill.

Mundane organizations and gardening

Paradoxically, the three modalities of action just mentioned, though lacking hope of any particular outcome, are the driving force for wider changes. The unobtrusive devotion of competent employees without any special aspirations, pessimists by reason but conscientious by vocation, enables organizations to function and adapt more than we could usually imagine. The pointless stubbornness of deviants who persist in their exploration of areas considered fruitless provides opportunities to discover hidden treasures. The patience and passivity of a Kutuzov, who does not think he can achieve anything important but has a far-reaching understanding of a situation, nurtures the morale of his troops, and seeks to avoid interfering with developments of history that might be favorable. This is the approach of a gardener rather than an engineer.

Engineers are helpless when deprived of a full understanding of the complex relationships of causality that govern phenomena and access to sufficient means of action and control. Gardeners accept this powerlessness in the face of the overwhelming forces of nature, but believe that they can nevertheless plant seeds at the appropriate time, pull up weeds regularly, and adapt their watering to the sunshine. These are the small, mundane actions that, performed with constancy, will ultimately yield more opportunities to foster the emergence of a world that is increasingly true, beautiful, and just.

APPENDIX 2

MUNDANE ORGANIZATIONS AND HEROIC LEADERS[1]

James G. March

i

Consider two simple questions about organizations and their leadership: First, what makes an organization function well? Second, what are managerial biases in dealing with the trade-offs involved in making organizations function well? The questions are simple; the answers are not; but I think we can say a few things.

There is a sizable industry devoted to producing books about leadership and optimal leadership styles. For the most part, such books portray relatively heroic attributes of leadership as producing relatively heroic consequences. Organizations, their historians, and particularly their leaders are inclined to personalize organizational histories and to endow particular leaders with implausibly profound impacts on the flow of events. In particular, in discussing organizations and their leadership, we are often led to grand proclamations about innovation, dramatic interventions, and heroic leadership. Although such things may be important, understanding

---

[1] These remarks were originally made on March 25, 1982, at a conference on university administration held at Mexicali, Mexico, and printed in Lewis B. Mayhew and Fernando Leon-Garcia (eds.), *Seminarios sobre administración universitaria* (Seminars on university administration). Centro de Enseñada Técnica y Superior, 1988. They were subsequently published (in French) as "Organisations prosaïques et leaders héroïques", *Gérer et Comprendre*, 60 (June 2000) 44–50.

what makes organizations work probably begins with recognizing the importance of lesser things.

No organization can work well if there are long lines of people waiting for something and letters and telephone calls that are unanswered, or if there are shortages of supplies, or if there are overlooked assignments. In our contemporary sophistication about the limits of elementary efficiency, we sometimes forget the simple fact that organizations cannot work well unless ordinary tasks are performed routinely and well. It must be obvious to us all that some organizations work well in such a sense and others do not.

Suppose, for example, that a visitor to the United States set out to observe the social and organizational response to an automobile accident. What such a visitor would discover was that the response differed considerably from one part of the country to another. Suppose there is an automobile accident in which several people are injured, and you observe what happens:

- If you are in Vermont, the people living in nearby houses will be watering their gardens, not wanting to appear to be interfering with other people's lives. So the accident victims will be lying there but they will not have their privacy disturbed.
- If you are in Florida, the people will be standing around weeping and consoling the victims, telling them how sorry they are that such a thing could have happened.
- If you are in New York, the people and the victims will be yelling at each other, arguing whose fault it is.
- If you are in California, the police will be on the scene along with paramedics, the most modern equipment, and a public psychiatrist to care for the witnesses' trauma.
- If you are in Iowa, the police will have arrived, but the victims will already have been taken to the nearest hospital by the residents in their own cars, and the neighbors will be cleaning the streets.

Each of these methods for organizing a response to an automobile accident has some beauty in it. But I want to argue that usually it is better to be organized in the last way, in the Iowa way, than in the others.

Organizing so that problems are handled quickly and more or less automatically by whoever is there requires certain general attributes within the culture, certain kinds of individual feelings within the organization, a distribution of individual competences, and some organizational arrangements.

It doesn't necessarily happen automatically, and it doesn't make many heroes.

Let me mention four components of elementary efficiency in organizations. They are neither novel nor mysterious; but they are, I believe, fundamental. The first of these, and I suspect the most important, is simple *competence*. Organizations work well if the people in them know what they are doing. How is competence encouraged? In some very traditional ways. It requires appointment and promotion on the basis of merit rather than personal ties or irrelevant characteristics. It requires a division of labor, specialization, routinization, and training. In short, competence requires that the people doing the work know what they are doing, and that people who don't know what they are doing are excluded or exclude themselves from doing the work.

A second component of elementary efficiency is *initiative*. Organizations work well if problems are attended to most of the time locally, promptly, and autonomously. This is accomplished by delegation accompanied by instincts or rules of tolerance. If you are going to encourage initiative, you need to be tolerant of small deviations from what you would do yourself in the same situation. Delegation implies the right to be wrong. You also need to build attention buffers so that not everyone sees everything. Just as parents learn not to notice everything their children are doing, organizations that want to encourage initiative learn not to notice small annoyances.

A third component of elementary efficiency is *identification*. Organizations work well if persons in them take pride in their work and in the organization. They have a sense of shared destiny, mutual trust, and collective identity. Identification is accomplished primarily by integrating personal work with organizational effort, by having a culture of cooperation supported by social norms and group sanctions, and by a sense of group cohesion and efficacy. It is often sustained, in part, by an external threat, by the perception of an enemy on the outside.

A fourth component of elementary efficiency is *unobtrusive coordination*. Organizations work well if the autonomous actions of individuals are coordinated effectively, quickly, and inexpensively. How is coordination accomplished? It is accomplished by routinization, by the development of standard operating procedures, by the flow of signals and information so that people know what is going on, by anticipation of individuals, and by redundancy.

These four things – competence, initiative, identification, and unobtrusive coordination – are very conventional. They are found in any standard book on administration. Because they are so conventional and so standard, many of us who think we are sophisticated sometimes act as though they are unimportant. In fact, competence, initiative, identification, and unobtrusive coordination, and decisions about them, are at the heart of effective leadership. They are not grand; they are not heroic; they are not – for the most part – even interesting. They suggest a view of leadership somewhat at variance with the view held by many managers and many books on organizational leadership.

ii

Leadership involves many things, and I will not attempt a list. Underlying many leadership skills is a basic one – the capability to use judgment informed by analysis and experience. Constructing good judgment from analysis and experience, however, is subject to error; leaders are not always right. Some of the errors that organizational leaders make are unsystematic in the sense that different leaders have different weaknesses, but there is no consistent relation between properties of leaders and the character of the errors in judgment that they make. Others of the errors, on the other hand, are more systematic.

In particular, there are some special features of the managerial role and the career path to it that lead to systematic leadership biases. The most conspicuous of these is the tendency for organizational leaders to have an overly grand vision of leadership and management and an exaggerated sense of their own importance. Like most of us, leaders want to believe in their own importance. Unlike most of us, they have plenty of casual evidence that they are important. The evidence may, however, be misleading.

As managers rise through an organization, managerial power is celebrated; the trappings of managerial importance are increased; but it becomes less clear that a leader's action has major effects on organizational performance. The loss of clarity is two fold as we move toward the top of an organization: Organizational objectives become more ambiguous, and the contributions of organizational leaders to performance become less clear. A symptom of this ambiguity is found in the tendency of managers (and those who depend on them or look up to them) to become sensitive to symbols of position and leadership. The procedures and dramas of decision are organized to emphasize the importance of management and managers, to reassure us of the significance of leaders. Information is gathered and reported to symbolize that decisions are made properly. Meetings are held to symbolize that specific actions have been decided upon by persons in authority. Control procedures are introduced to symbolize that the system is controlled. Evaluations are used to symbolize that managers are monitoring the organization properly.

As a result of these rituals and ceremonies, it seems very likely that most *organizational leaders exaggerate their control over their successes.* We know that individuals tend to exaggerate the importance of individual action in controlling human events and that this exaggeration is particularly common among people who have been successful. Successful people tend to imagine that the events of their lives are produced by their actions. Organizational leaders are systematically successful. The managers we see in an organization are typically people who have risen to their present positions by being evaluated as successes in previous positions. Such successes encourage them to see their own histories as the consequences of their own actions and competences.

This powerful belief on the part of successful people, the idea that their successes are the product of their competences, qualities, and efforts, is not particularly supported by research on managerial success. Studies of success in organizations shows that successful people in most organizations, as in most other walks of life, are distinguished particularly by having made two early decisions very well: The first decision is the choice of parents; people who choose successful parents are much more likely to be successful themselves than are those who are unwise enough to choose unsuccessful parents. The second early decision is the choice of gender; people who decide to be male are much more likely to be successful managers than are those who decide to be female. These two "decisions" do not, of course, account for everything; far from it; but they account for more than any other two things that we know.

Once you leave such well-known attributes of organizational leaders, research on managerial success provides very few consistent results. Most measured attributes of leaders fail to predict success with any accuracy. It is possible that the research is deficient. Undoubtedly it is. There may well be some interactions between attributes of leaders and attributes of leadership situations that account for success. However, it seems to me that most writers on leadership and most leaders probably overestimate the extent to which managerial success is produced by managers. Perhaps after we screen out the obviously inappropriate people, as we are likely to do rather early in a managerial promotion ladder, we cannot really distinguish one vice president from another.

It seems likely that organizational leaders will *confuse indispensability, which they cannot claim, with importance, which they may*. As a consequence of the hierarchically arranged series of organizational evaluations that are made as leaders compete for promotion, the pool of leaders eligible for further promotion becomes increasingly homogeneous toward the top of an organization. Managers look more and more alike in attitudes, competences, energies, and commitments. At the same time, as we move up the organization, objectives become more ambiguous and the connection between the actions of leaders and organizational outcomes more tenuous. As a result, the evaluation of leaders becomes subject to more random error. At the limit, the error variance in the evaluation procedures exceeds the variation within the pool of eligible leaders; and we cannot distinguish one leader from another.

In a properly functioning organization, therefore, top level managers may well be useful, even essential; but since they are not distinguishable, no individual manager is indispensable. It is natural for an organizational leader to want to be indispensable, to yearn for confirmation that he or she is uniquely important, rather than just important. But where we find such leaders, it is a symptom of an ineffective organization. In an effective organization, we won't be able to tell one vice-president from another.

iii

The contrast between the elementary things that make an organization work and heroic conceptions of leadership is striking. It is also potentially unsettling for leaders. Acknowledgment of the relative unimportance of leadership heroics is inconsistent with their interpretations of their own experiences. They do not want it to be true, and they do not believe it to be true. As a result, they overlook some things that seem to me quite fundamental to understanding how organizations work.

First, *organizations work because of a density of ordinary competence throughout the organization*. The German Army was an effective army not because of its generals, although its generals were competent, but because of the capability of many German sergeants to act effectively and autonomously. They knew how to do what needed to be done. Specialization is a useful and powerful tool in organizing; but if we have to call a specialist to fix anything that goes wrong in an organization, most things won't work most of the time. Organizations that work are those in which if someone sees a toilet not working, he or she fixes it; and that is hard to accomplish unless the ability to do the elementary things that organizations require is widely available throughout the organization.

Second, *organizations work because subunits and individuals are interdependently autonomous.* That is, they are left alone to do their jobs. There is mutual delegation and mutual confidence. Work is coordinated in a relatively unobtrusive manner, less by explicit interventions than by mutual anticipations. I know what you're going to do; you know what I'm going to do; we don't have to talk much about it. Coordination is accomplished by informal arrangements and by slack buffers that keep us from interfering with each other. It is accomplished by unobtrusive signals and information flows. In short, organizations work better when organizational management is more like sailing than power boating.

Third, *organizations work well because they have redundancy.* Almost everyone is important but no one is indispensable, either over time or at a given point. If a task needs to be done, there are several individuals, technologies, and routines available to do it. The task does not depend critically on any one person or unit. Redundancy in organizations, as in mechanical equipment, often looks expensive; it is tempting to reduce it; but without redundancy organizations are vulnerable to failure if any individual part fails; and that likelihood increases rapidly with increasing scale and complexity of organizational operations.

Fourth, *organizations work because they have mutual trust without personal favoritism.* Classic forms of trust, in families for example, are associated with favoritism. An organization requires a different form of trust, not confidence in mutual personal support but confidence that a job will be done well and with understanding of the job requirements of others. Particularly in the relations between superiors and subordinates, where there is a good deal of mutual dependence, trust is valuable; but the temptations of personal favoritism are strong.

Because of the ways in which we write and think about organizational leadership, and because of the personal success experience by which we prepare individuals for leadership, these mundane truisms about organizations are likely to be forgotten by leaders as they look for dramatic ways to make their marks upon an organization.

iv

Suppose that the beliefs of organizational leaders were to become different. Suppose they accepted the proposition that most of what makes an organization work well is mundane rather than heroic and that however important leadership may be to an organization, no individual leader is very important. If leaders were to believe such a story, what would keep them from surrendering to self-pity, cynicism, and withdrawal? If hope for grand consequences is denied them, how do leaders sustain the commitment and drive that we expect and perhaps need from them? How does a senior manager who doubts his own significance justify action and involvement?

Since the question of dealing with human insignificance is a classic one, the answer is more properly sought in classic texts than in studies of organizations. We face a world in which the things that make an organization work are prosaic things; we face a world in which it is hard to discover whether what we do makes a difference. We ask what we might say to a modern leader. As a start, we might suggest that leaders read *War and Peace*. Perhaps time spent examining General Kutuzov's ruminations at the Battle of Borodino would be more valuable than time spent studying strategic planning. Certainly, Tolstoy's discussion of the complications of being a general when one doubts the efficacy of generalship exhibits greater understanding of the ambiguities of leadership than do most modern writings on organizations.

Or we might recommend Ibsen. In *The Wild Duck*, Ibsen has Dr. Relling warn us that if we take the illusions away from an ordinary person, we take away happiness at the same time. Dr. Relling's warning is echoed elsewhere in literature, notably by O'Neil and Pirandello; and it is far from foolish. In our rush to sophisticated doubt about the possibilities for intentional action, we should not ignore the extent to which an innocent belief in heroic consequences can sustain commitment to fulfill the demands of leadership.

However, I want to remind you of yet another classic answer. Consider the words of Don Quixote as he explains himself to Don Diego de Miranda: "I am not as mad or as foolish as I must have seemed to you . . . All knights have their own endeavors . . . since it is my fortune to be counted in the number of knights errant, I cannot help but attack all things that seem to me to fall within the jurisdiction of my endeavors" (II, 17).

Quixote's statement embraces a view of life and action that uncouples heroic commitment from great hopes for consequences. It speaks of obligations rather than expectations, of a life that is to be lived and enjoyed, and of duties that are to be honored. Cervantes encourages charging at windmills, not out of confusion about what windmills are but out of enthusiasm for life and an understanding of the demands of an identity.

If I can extrapolate unreasonably from Cervantes to the ordinary world of organizations, I think that Quixote tells an organizational leader that good leadership combines an exuberance for life with a commitment to the prosaic duties of leadership; that leadership is poetry and routine as well as action; that it is beauty as well as truth, the appreciation of complexity as well as simplicity, the pursuit of contradiction as well as coherence, the achievement of grace as well as control. The verbiage seems much too romantic for a cynical age, and yet some recent observations of organizations suggest that such a vision may be more common than we realize.

If leaders acted in Quixote's spirit, they would enrich our lives and improve our organizations. They would manage the mundane things that make organizations work, and they would produce decisions, actions, and lives that could be read and interpreted as poetry. Such leadership involves keeping the toilets working. It also involves writing pieces of managerial poetry – documents, memoranda, reports, and orders – that stimulate new and interesting interpretations and implementations. And in the best of all worlds, perhaps, a leader might say of the organizational interpretation of a command what T. S. Eliot once wrote about the interpretation of one of his poems: "[the] analysis was an attempt to find out what the poem meant, whether that was what I had meant it to mean or not. And for that I was grateful."[2]

---

[2]   T. S. Eliot, *On poetry and poets*, New York: Noonday, 1961, 125–6, reprinting a piece entitled "The frontiers of criticism" (1956).

INDEX